The
WORST-CASE SCENARIO
Survival Handbook:
DATING & SEX

The
WORST-CASE SCENARIO
Survival Handbook:
DATING & SEX

By Joshua Piven, David Borgenicht, and Jennifer Worick
Illustrations by Brenda Brown

CHRONICLE BOOKS

SAN FRANCISCO

Copyright © 2001 by Quirk Productions, Inc.

All rights reserved. No part of this book may be reproduced in any form without written permission from the publisher.

Worst-Case Scenario™ and The Worst-Case Scenario Survival Handbook™ are trademarks of Quirk Productions, Inc.

Library of Congress Cataloging-in-Publication Data available.

ISBN: 0-8118-3241-4

Printed in the United States

Typeset in Adobe Caslon, Bundesbahn Pi, and Zapf Dingbats

Designed by Frances J. Soo Ping Chow
Illustrations by Brenda Brown

A **QUIRK** Book
www.quirkproductions.com
Visit www.worstcasescenarios.com

Distributed in Canada by Raincoast Books
9050 Shaughnessy Street
Vancouver, BC V6P 6E5

10 9 8 7 6 5 4 3

Chronicle Books LLC
85 Second Street
San Francisco, California 94105
www.chroniclebooks.com

WARNING

When a dire situation is at hand, safe and sane alternatives may not exist. To deal with the worst-case dating and sex scenarios presented in this book, we highly recommend—insist, actually—that you carefully evaluate the situation before you act; that you act responsibly, safely, and within the boundaries of the law; and that you attempt to consult a professionally trained expert, therapist, or physician before placing yourself in harm's way. However, because highly trained professionals may not always be available when the physical or emotional well-being and safety of individuals is at risk, we have asked experts on various subjects to describe the techniques they might employ in these emergency dating situations. THE PUBLISHER, AUTHORS, AND EXPERTS DISCLAIM ANY LIABILITY from any harm or injury—physical or emotional—that may result from the use, proper or improper, of the information contained in this book. We do not claim that the information contained herein is going to be complete, safe, or accurate for the specific situation you may find yourself in. Moreover, it should by no means be considered a substitute for your good judgement and common sense. And finally, nothing in this book should be construed or interpreted to infringe on the rights of other persons nor to encourage you to violate criminal statutes: all activities described should be conducted by consenting adults and in accord with all state and federal laws. Breaking a heart is one thing—breaking the law is another.

—The Authors

The course of true love never did run smooth.
—William Shakespeare

CONTENTS

4 Bedroom Survival Skills...103

INTRODUCTION

In nature, the process of finding a mate is a fairly simple one. Animals signal their readiness by fanning their plumage, or changing the color of their buttocks, or growling in a certain way. Potential suitors present themselves, then vie for the right to mate. In nature, there are no singles bars, personal ads, safe lunches, or blind dates.

Among humans, however, finding a suitable mate is a lot more complex, and more dangerous. From the first attraction across a crowded room to the perils of meeting, dating, undressing, sleeping with, and loving or leaving that special someone, you are completely at risk: your body, your heart, your mind, and your spirit, not to mention your bank account. Literature and lyrics say it all: Love hurts. Love is blind. Love stinks. Love is a battlefield.

Think of this book as your guide to fighting, surviving, and ultimately winning that battle.

We've learned a few things about survival in writing *The Worst-Case Scenario Survival Handbook* and *The Worst-Case Scenario Survival Handbook: Travel.* We've learned how to fend off an alligator, how to survive a jump from a bridge, how to escape from quicksand, and how to survive many other life-threatening situations.

That was the easy part.

It was easy to give readers instructions for surviving the elements or wild animal attacks. It's simple enough to predict what a shark is going to do, or to teach people how to jump from a moving car, or to give readers information about what to do during an earthquake. Sharks are always going to behave like sharks, moving cars are always going to function according to the principles of physics, and earthquakes affect the ground and buildings in a very predictable way.

But human nature is much less predictable than Mother Nature.

In dating and sex, perhaps more than in any other aspect of life, you've got to be able to cope when things don't work out as planned. If you are careless or you panic, if you say or do the wrong thing or do the right thing at the wrong time, the consequences could be emotionally catastrophic and life-threatening, or life-producing. This book can keep you safe.

There are plenty of books out there that provide guidance on how to find Mr. or Ms. Right. This is the only book that tells you how to escape from Mr. or Ms. Wrong. Identify an axe murderer, slip away from a bad date, survive when your credit card is declined, fake an orgasm, recognize breast implants and toupees, remove difficult articles of clothing—*The Worst-Case Scenario Survival Handbook: Dating & Sex* can save your evening and your love life.

Once again, we've assembled a team of experts to give real advice and tips about what to do when good dates (and relationships) go bad. We've consulted with sex therapists, etiquette instructors, CIA and FBI agents, lawyers, bartenders, psychologists, emergency medical instructors, nutritionists, college professors, barbers, fashion consultants, dermatologists, and dozens of other professionals who have generously lent us their knowledge and experience in order to give you the information you'll need to survive the treacherous dating and sex scenarios that follow.

You'll find out how to survive dozens of physically and emotionally threatening situations in bars, restaurants, bedrooms, and airplane lavatories. And in the handy appendix, you'll find excuses you might need, a guide to pickup lines to avoid, and a body language interpretation chart for encouragement—or for extra protection.

We've added a new, female member to our team of authors, to make sure we cover all the bases. Generally, we've assigned a "he" or "she" to each of the scenarios for the sake of simplicity, but you'll know if the scenario applies to you. And even if it doesn't, you might find out how to help a friend or lover in distress.

So go out, have fun, and carry this book at all times—because you just never know.

—Joshua Piven, David Borgenicht, and Jennifer Worick

CHAPTER 1

DEFENSIVE DATING

HOW TO DETERMINE IF YOUR DATE IS AN AXE MURDERER

1 Watch for the following:
- A Caucasian male in his twenties or thirties
- Obsession with fire or matches
- Cruelty to animals
- History of bed-wetting
- Sexually abused as a child
- Middle-class background combined with loner behavior
- Difficulty maintaining relationships

An individual who exhibits more than three of these traits may be dangerous.

2 Trust your intuition.
Your instinct is a powerful weapon. If something feels wrong, it probably is.

3 Check him out officially.
Obtain his social security number and investigate him. Call the Federal Prison Locator Service (202-307-3126) to determine if he was ever incarcerated. Many online companies can aid in financial reports or tracking down previous addresses. You may also want to enlist the services of a private detective.

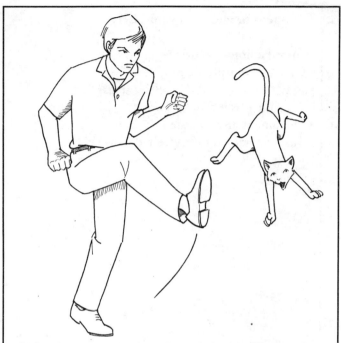

Axe murderers are usually Caucasian males in their twenties and thirties. They frequently behave cruelly toward animals and may also be obsessed with fire or matches.

4 If you discover grounds for suspicion, break off the relationship immediately.

Be clear and definite about your decision. Return all of his belongings and gifts. Do not make promises to keep in touch. Be straightforward and kind, and talk only about yourself and why the relationship no longer works for you. Do not blame him. Try not to make him angry.

5 Take steps to maintain your safety.
- Carry a cell phone.
- Install a home security system.
- Change your phone numbers.
- Stay near populated, well-lit areas.
- Apprise a friend or relative of your concerns.
- Document any strange or unusual happenings.
- Take a personal safety/self-defense class.

HOW TO
DETERMINE IF YOUR
DATE IS MARRIED

1   Examine the left ring finger.
After a period of about one year, a wedding band leaves a circle of lighter skin around the base of the ring finger. Your date may also touch the base of that finger inadvertently, as if something is missing.

2   Ask for a home phone number.
Most people in committed relationships spend at least one or two hours a week on the phone; if your date will not give you his home phone number, then he is worried someone else will answer when you call.

3   Insist on holding hands when walking in public.
If your date is interested and attracted to you, then he will not object to such a small and commonplace display of affection—unless he fears that someone will spot you together.

4   Search your date's car.
The automobile registration may be in the spouse's name, or in both names. It is usually kept in the glove compartment, behind the sun visor or, for non-smokers, in the ashtray. Look for signs of a spouse (clothing, makeup) or other indicators (pacifiers, pieces of crackers, toys) of a family your date has not mentioned.

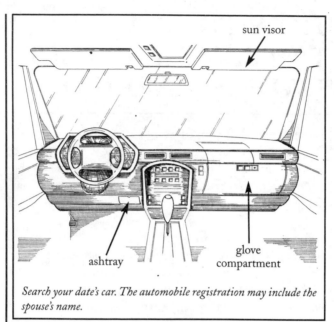

Search your date's car. The automobile registration may include the spouse's name.

5 Ask to meet some of his friends.

After two or three dates, this is not an unusual request. If your date claims that his friends remain close to his ex-wife, or that it's too soon to bring you into their social circle, you have good reason to believe that you are not the only woman in his life.

6 Invite him to spend the night.

If you have engaged in sexual activity on several occasions but he always refuses to stay the night, then he very likely has someone waiting for him.

7 Make plans to spend a weekend together.
If you never see him on Saturdays and Sundays, be suspicious. Your date may say that he spends weekends with his parents and/or with his children. But if he cares so much for you, and if his family is as great as he says they are, they will understand if you come along or if he shares time on the weekends with you.

8 Ask to meet his children.
He might have legitimate reasons for not introducing you to his children early in the relationship—for example, he may not want to present you as a possible mommy replacement until the relationship becomes more serious. However, it may also mean he is still married to their mommy.

Be Aware
Be suspicious of a lover who never writes you letters or sends e-mails, and signs greeting cards with only a nickname, an initial, or a term of endearment. This person may be making a conscious effort to avoid any paper trails to the relationship. For this same reason, also be wary of a date who always pays cash (see "How to Have an Affair and Not Get Caught," page 142).

HOW TO DETERMINE THE GENDER OF YOUR DATE

1 | **Look at her (or his) hand.**
Compare the length of your date's fourth and second fingers. Most men have ring fingers that are conspicuously longer than their index fingers, whereas most women have ring fingers that are close to the same length. Testosterone levels likely account for the greater length.

Also take notice of the amount of hair on your date's knuckles, hands, and forearms. Most men will have visible, dark hair (or signs of recently removed hair) on their hands and wrists, and sometimes knuckles.

2 | **Be suspicious of baggy clothing.**
Your date may be trying to conceal a telltale bulge.

3 | **Look for an Adam's apple.**
Most men have a bump in the middle of their throat. Most women do not.

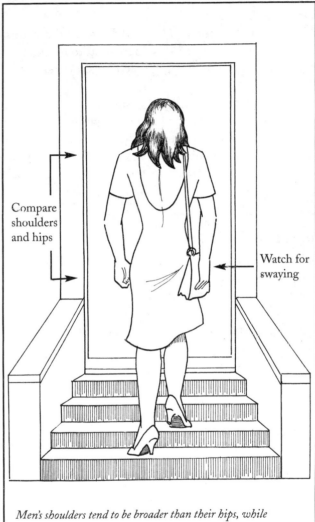

Compare shoulders and hips

Watch for swaying

Men's shoulders tend to be broader than their hips, while women's hips and shoulders tend to be closer to the same width. When ascending stairs, women tend to sway more than men.

4 Observe shoulders and hips.
Men's shoulders tend to be broader than their hips, while women's hips and shoulders tend to be closer to the same width. Do not be fooled by shoulder pads.

5 Follow your date up a flight of stairs.
Take note of how she (or he) moves while ascending. Men tend to walk in a more "straight ahead" motion with minimal "wobbling" back and forth. Women tend to sway a bit from side to side, due to the position of their pelvises. Women also tend to lean forward slightly.

Be Aware

- Look for at least three of these characteristics before you draw conclusions about your date's gender, then make your plans accordingly.
- Voice is not always a good indicator of gender—a low voice may simply be the result of hard living.

HOW TO DETERMINE IF YOUR DATE IS A CON ARTIST

1 Watch for the following:
- Has your date missed a string of dates with you?
- Does she change dates at the last minute?
- Does she frequently receive unexplained phone calls?
- Does she refuse to give out information about her past?
- Is she known only by a first or last name?
- Is she loath to contact family members?
- Does she lack connections to the community, friends, or co-workers?
- Does she frequently express concerns about her finances?
- Has she ever asked you for a short-term loan or investment?
- Does she often change her stories and claims?

If the answer to three or more of these questions is yes, you may be dating a con artist (or a pathological liar).

2 Watch your date's eyes during conversation.
Most people look to their right when recalling the truth, the past, and events that actually happened. People look to the left when "creating" or spinning out new versions of past events. Ask her a question about her past and see where her eyes move.

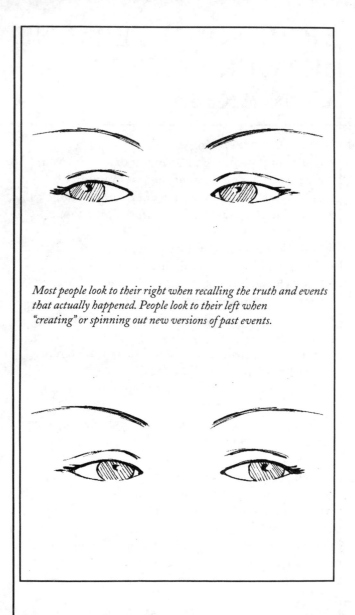

Most people look to their right when recalling the truth and events that actually happened. People look to their left when "creating" or spinning out new versions of past events.

3 | Obtain her social security number and investigate her records.

With a social security number or driver's license number and birthdate, you can check out a person's records—criminal, financial, voting, and more. A good place to start is a "people finder" website on the Internet. Or you can hire a private detective.

4 | Trust your intuition.

If you have doubts, there is probably a reason.

5 | Protect yourself.

Take an inventory of your credit cards, bank accounts, and other financial assets. If you have broken off the relationship and she is desperate, she may try to dupe or rob you. Request new credit cards; change your e-mail, voicemail, burglar alarm, and banking passwords; select a new PIN for each of your accounts. Change your locks, if necessary.

HOW TO FEND OFF AN OBSESSIVE EX

1 Make your rejection final and firm.
Do not give your ex a chance to manipulate or negotiate. Refuse all offers for dates, favors, and "friendly meetings." Express your wish to be left alone. Make sure your body language sends the same message. Do not touch during the rejection, but look your ex firmly in the eyes.

2 Do not discuss the past.
Never mention the good times you had together. Instead, speak enthusiastically about how happy you are now, and make it clear that you have moved on with your life.

3 Immediately sever all ties.
Return all of your ex's belongings (including any gifts to you) in one shipment. Do not prolong the process. If your ex continues to call, get a new, unlisted phone number. Do not call or send cards, letters, or e-mails; these will result in a mixed message and may give your ex hope of reconciliation.

4 If your ex will not leave you alone, sound a warning.
At the first sign that your ex is not listening to you, announce that if the unwanted behavior persists, you will take action. Threaten to contact the authorities, and be prepared to do so. Do not give in to any threats that may come your way. Be ready to secure

a restraining order or civil protection order if it becomes necessary for your peace of mind.

5 Inform your family, friends, and co-workers about the situation.
Having larger, stronger friends around may serve as a deterrent.

6 Keep a paper trail.
You may need evidence later. Save any relevant letters, notes, e-mails, and voicemails—anything that can prove unwanted attention. Maintain a log or diary of your ex's actions and report any unlawful behavior to the police immediately. Report phone calls from your ex to both the phone company and the police. Write down your caller ID log, if you have one.

7 Inform the authorities.
Do not let fear of retribution stop you from taking action. If your ex persists in contacting you, becomes easily enraged by your rejections, is overly interested in your private life, or shows up in unexpected locations, he or she has become a stalker. Take legal action immediately and obtain a restraining order.

8 Move.
Make sure that your new address is unlisted. Contact the department of motor vehicles and the voter registration bureau to have them block your address. Forward your mail to a P.O. box, and do not accept any packages unless you are certain who sent them.

9 Take steps to preserve your safety.
Get a cell phone and carry it with you at all times.
Consider getting a guard dog and taking self-defense
classes.

Be Aware
If your ex shows up where you work, notify co-
workers of the situation and vary the times you
come and go from work. If possible, have someone
accompany you as you approach the building.

HOW TO FEND OFF A PICKUP ARTIST

1 | Recognize the traits of a pickup artist.
Is your suitor overly charming and quick with cash? Does he appear to have an immediate connection with you? Is he scanning the room while talking to you? Is he calling you familiar or condescending names such as "honey," "sweetie," or "babe"?

2 | Do not accept drinks.
Letting a pickup artist buy you drinks will encourage him and make him feel he is entitled to your attentions.

3 | Keep personal information to yourself.
Do not give him your name, and do not tell him where you live, who you are waiting for, or any other detail or insight into your personal life or plans.

4 | Make it clear that you are not interested.
Be direct and forceful. If he persists, you may have to become rude or leave. If you make it obvious that nothing is going to happen that evening, he'll move on to other prospects.

5 | Turn away and ignore him.
Talk to a friend or the person sitting on the other side of you. The pickup artist likes the chase most of all— put a stop to the chase and he will look elsewhere.

The Elbow Knock: Turn back to glance at the pickup artist and sweep your elbow toward the glass.

The Time Check: Turn your wrist to look at your watch, and spill your drink on the pickup artist.

6 Cause an "accident."

- The Elbow Knock: Use this technique if you are seated at a bar or table. Notice where glasses and plates are located on your table. Turn around to talk to a friend, or simply look away, and position your elbow. As you turn back, sweep your elbow into any glasses or plates on the table, knocking them into his lap or onto his shirt.

- The Hair Flip: While standing facing your suitor, bring your hand up to adjust your hair. Do this quickly so that he tips his glass toward his body and his drink spills all over him.

- The Time Check: While standing next to your would-be suitor, hold your drink in the hand of your watch arm. Say, "Is it [*time*] yet?" Then turn your wrist to look at your watch, thereby spilling the drink on the pickup artist.

7 Apologize insincerely.

HOW TO DEAL WITH A DATE WHO MOVES TOO FAST

1 Watch for the signs of "relationship acceleration."
If your date starts talking about moving in or having kids or marrying, and you are not yet ready to proceed that quickly, you may have a problem.

2 Tell your date to slow down.
Send a clear, unambiguous message. Sometimes joking about it will convey your feelings, but if a light touch does not work, express it more directly: tell him that you think he is getting too serious too soon, and that you think you both should spend time with other friends.

3 Do not agree to more than one date a week.
By no means should you plan a weekend vacation together.

4 Talk about past relationships.
Find out what goals he had in recent relationships. Someone who moves at a lightning pace may be on the rebound, wanting only to replace a past relationship. Be sure you are not being used merely as a vehicle for accomplishing a goal that you were not involved in setting, like having kids or buying a house.

5 | **Postpone any conversation about the future of your relationship.**
If you want to continue dating this person but do not want to get serious yet, suggest discussing the situation at a specific date in the future, after you have spent some more time together.

6 | **Beware of flattery.**
When someone wants to move too fast, he may just be lonely or incapable of being single. You may feel flattered by his seriousness, but often his intensity does not have much to do with you. He may only want to be with someone, anyone.

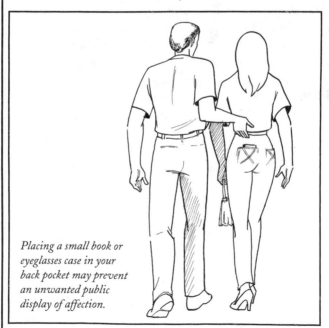

Placing a small book or eyeglasses case in your back pocket may prevent an unwanted public display of affection.

How to Stop Unwanted PDAs

Overeager dates may use a Public Display of Affection (PDA) to accelerate a relationship, unaware that these PDAs may make you, your friends, or even casual bystanders feel uncomfortable. The best solution is to voice discomfort—but because that can be awkward, use the following techniques to block an unwanted PDA:

- Handholding: If your date tries to hold your hand, allow him to do so for a few minutes, release the hand to adjust your hair, and then lower the hand to your side. Alternative: You could fake a sneeze, then lower both hands to your sides.
- Kissing: As your date advances, step back and explain you're catching a cold. Sound concerned for your date's health and well-being. Alternative: Sneeze or cough in his face.
- Walking with One Hand Slipped in the Rear Pocket of Your Pants: Pull your date's hand out of your pocket, perhaps with a coy line like, "Wait until we get home." Alternative: Place an object—a checkbook, a wallet, a folded scarf, a glasses case, or a rolled newspaper—in the pocket.

HOW TO ESCAPE FROM A BAD DATE

FAKE AN EMERGENCY

1 Excuse yourself from the table.
Tell your date that you are going to the restroom to "wash up." Take your cell phone with you. If you do not have one, locate a restaurant phone that's out of your date's line of vision. Bring a restaurant matchbook or a business card that includes the restaurant's phone number.

2 Call a friend or relative for help.
Tell them to call you (either on your cell phone or on the restaurant's phone) and pretend there has been an emergency. Believable emergencies are:
- Personal Crisis: "My friend just broke up with her husband—she's having a breakdown. I have to go."
- Business Crisis: "My boss just called—she's in Seattle for a major presentation, and has lost all her files. I have to e-mail them to her immediately."
- Health Crisis: "My sister just called—our grandmother is alone and ill."

3 Leave quickly before your date can protest.
Apologize, but refuse any attempt your date makes to accompany you. If you leave swiftly and without hesitation, your date won't have time to understand what's happening or to object.

Slip Away Unnoticed

1 Identify your escape route.
Observe your surroundings. Take note of the exits, especially the back doors. Look for the best way out and an alternative.

2 Plan to alter your appearance.
Think about your most distinctive features and figure out how to hide or disguise them. The person you are trying to leave is going to see a figure moving past and away at a distance and will be focusing on the first impression. If you are not familiar to him and are uninteresting, you will not get a second look.

3 Excuse yourself from the table.
Move to the restroom or any private area with a mirror to begin your transformation. Your date will probably wait only two or three minutes before expecting you to return, so act quickly, before he begins looking for you.

4 Add or remove clothing.
Layering garments will change your body shape and even suggest a different gender. A long coat will obscure your body type. Hats are especially useful because they conceal your hair and facial features. Eyeglasses, whether added or removed, work wonders. A shopping bag is a handy prop and can be used to hold your belongings.

Add—or remove—eyeglasses. Roll or unroll your sleeves; tuck in or untuck your blouse. Modify your hairstyle.

5 | **Change your walk and posture.**
If you usually walk quickly, move slowly. If you stand up straight, hunch over. To alter your gait, slip a pebble in one shoe or bind one of your knees with a piece of string or cloth.

6 | **Use or remove cosmetics.**
Lipstick can change the shape of your mouth, heighten the color in your cheeks and nose, and even give you tired eyes if dabbed and blended on your eyelids. An eyebrow pencil can be used to add age lines, change the shape of your eyes and brows, or create facial hair.

7 | **Change your hairstyle or color.**
A rubberband, hairspray, water, or any gooey substance can be useful for changing a hairstyle, darkening your hair, or altering a hairline. Borrow flour from the kitchen to lighten or gray your hair color.

8 | **Adopt a cover role.**
A waiter in the restaurant may have an apron and be carrying a tray. If you can manage to procure these items, add or subtract a pair of eyeglasses and alter your hairline or hairstyle, you can become invisible as you are moving out of the restaurant, into the kitchen, and out the rear door. Or you can take on the role of a maintenance worker; carry a convenient potted plant out the front door and no one will think twice.

9 | **Make your move.**
Do not look at your date.

SLIP OUT THE WINDOW

If you do not think you will be able to change your appearance enough to slip past your date, you may have to find another way to depart. Back doors are the simplest; they are often located near the restrooms or are marked as fire exits. Do not open an emergency exit door if it is alarmed unless absolutely necessary; an alarm will only draw attention. If there are no accessible alternate doors, you will need to find a window.

1 Locate a usable window.
Avoid windows with chicken wire or large plate glass. Bathroom windows often work best. If you are not on the ground floor, be sure there is a fire escape.

2 Attempt to open the window.
Do not immediately break the window, no matter how dire your need to get out.

3 Prepare to break the window if you cannot open it.
Make sure no one is around. If you can, lock the bathroom door.

4 Find an implement to break the window.
Try to avoid using your elbow, fist, or foot. Suitable implements are:
• Wastebasket
• Toilet plunger
• Handbag or briefcase
• Paper towel dispenser

Strike the center of the glass with the implement.

5 Strike the center of the glass with the implement.
If the hand holding the implement will come within
a foot of the window as you break it, wrap it with a
jacket or sweater before attempting to break the glass.
If no implement is available, use your heavily wrapped
hand; be sure you wrap your arm as well, beyond the
elbow.

6 | Punch out any remaining shards of glass.
Cover your fist with a jacket or sweater before removing the glass.

7 | Make your escape.
Do not worry about any minor nicks and cuts. Run.

Get Your Date to Leave

1 | Say something offensive.
If you know your date is of a particular religion or ethnicity, make inappropriate comments.

2 | Behave inappropriately.
Do things that you think he will find unattractive or distasteful: chew with your mouth open, eat with your fingers, argue with the waiter, close your eyes and pretend to sleep, light matches and drop them on your plate, ignore everything he says, and/or call someone else on your cell phone.

3 | Send your date on a "fool's errand."
- Tell him you want to go to a specific nightclub, but explain that it gets very crowded and that if you are not in line by a certain time (say, fifteen minutes from then), you won't get in. Tell your date that you have arranged to have your friend stop by the restaurant with guest passes, but that if your date does not go ahead to the nightclub to get in line, you'll never make it inside. If your date wants your cell phone number, give the number

willingly but make sure you change one digit. Promise you will see your date within half an hour. Never show.

- Fake an allergy attack, and insist that he leave in search of the appropriate over-the-counter allergy medicine. Explain that you must have been allergic to something in the drink/appetizer/food/taxicab, and that if you do not obtain your medicine you will break out in hives. When your date dutifully leaves, slip away.

Be Aware

Blind dates are the riskiest form of dating—it is best to check out a potential suitor extensively before the date.

- Have a friend agree to check out your potential suitor and call you before you enter the bar/restaurant. Send your friend in with a cell phone. Situate yourself at a bar nearby, and await her call. Have her contact you when she has identified the mark.
- If you discover unsavory facts about someone you're supposed to meet, call immediately to cancel the date. Blame work and say that you have to stay late at the office, or say that you're experiencing car trouble. A more permanent solution is to say that an old flame has reentered your life; this will prevent your blind date from calling you again and asking for a rain check.

CHAPTER 2
FIRST IMPRESSIONS

HOW TO SPOT A FAKE

BREAST IMPLANTS

1 **Remember: if they look too good to be true, they probably are.**

If a woman is over thirty and her breasts defy gravity without a bra or she has a strikingly full and firm upper cleavage and bosom, chances are her breasts are not fully natural. You should also be suspicious of breasts that sit very high on a woman's chest; this is another good sign of implants.

2 **Assess breast size as compared to frame size.**

Most, though not all, petite women have naturally small breasts.

3 **Be suspicious of baseball-shaped breasts or strangely arranged breasts.**

In cases of a poor augmentation, the outline of the implant may be noticeable, or the breast may have a very firm, round, baseball-like appearance. Poorly placed implants can often be seen through tight tops. While a good augmentation procedure can be difficult to detect by visual inspection alone, a bad one is quite noticeable.

4 **Check cleavage for rippling of the skin.**

Implants may ripple in the cleavage or on top of the breasts; look for a wave pattern across the surface.

If a woman is over thirty and has strikingly full breasts that sit very high on her chest, you have reason to be suspicious.

Natural breasts, even very large breasts, although soft, will never have a rippled appearance.

5 | **If appropriate, brush up against or hug someone with suspected breast implants.**
If her breasts feel firmer than normal, implants may be in use.

6 | **Check under and around the breast for scarring.**
In an intimate situation, the opportunity may arise for a closer visual and tactile inspection. Look for scarring under the breasts, around the nipple, and in the armpit area.

TOUPEES

1 Look for uneven hair texture.

Since toupees do not cover the entire scalp like a wig does, there will always be a place where the real hair meets the purchased hairpiece. Generally, men who wear toupees have thinning hair, so look for a patch of thick hair surrounded by areas with thinner coverage.

2 Beware of an abnormally thick patch of hair on the top of the scalp.

Toupees are very thick in order to effectively cover the nylon or fabric cap that is attached to the scalp.

3 Watch for inconsistent coloring.

Toupees generally do not perfectly match the color of the hair surrounding them. A very dark area of hair surrounded by thinner, lighter hair may indicate a toupee.

4 Note any shifting of hair on the scalp.

Toupees are usually attached to the scalp with wig tape or special adhesive, which can come loose, especially during high winds or excessive perspiration. A patch of hair that has moved or is out of place is a sure sign of a toupee.

5 Test your theory.

Reach for your date's head, saying, "You've got something in your hair." If he reacts quickly to stop you from touching his hair, you may have found a toupee.

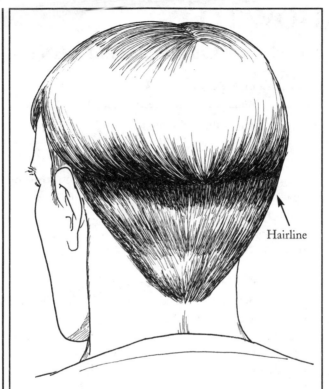

Hairline

Because toupees do not cover the entire scalp, there will always be a place where the real hair meets the purchased hairpiece.

Be Aware
Many men with thinning hair choose hair plugs, which are hair follicles that have been surgically implanted in the scalp. Lots of small bumps that resemble knots at the base of the hair shafts are a good indicator of hair plugs.

HOW TO SURVIVE A FASHION EMERGENCY

Shirt Caught in Zipper

1 Grasp the shirttail.
For internal snags, slide your hand inside the front of the pants above the zipper area. Otherwise, hold the material that is sticking out.

2 Pull the stuck fabric taut and upward.

3 Guide the zipper down with your free hand.
Apply steady force to the zipper: pull but don't yank too hard. Be careful not to pinch your fingers. Also, be sure to keep the garment away from the body, so the teeth of the zipper don't bite your skin. This is especially important if you're not wearing underwear.

Splashed by a Taxi

- If you are splashed with water, head for the nearest restroom and use the hot-air hand dryer. Stand very close to the dryer and rock from side to side, using your hands to billow and fluff whichever garment is wet.
- If you are splattered with mud, add a dash of salt to a glass of club soda from the closest bar and dab

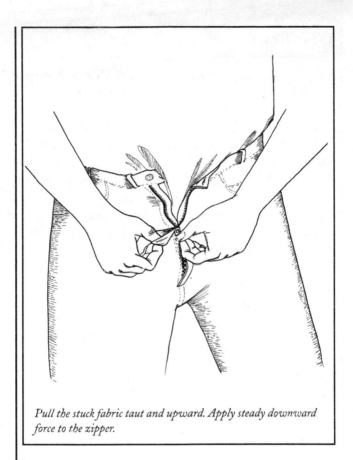

Pull the stuck fabric taut and upward. Apply steady downward force to the zipper.

it onto the dirty spots. The soda will work on the mud; the salt will lift out any oil from the street that was mixed in with the mud.

- If you are wearing a skirt, turn it around so that the splash is less visible. Untuck a shirt or blouse to cover a splashed skirt or pants.

Wine Stain

- For white wine, wet a cloth napkin with cold water and dab the stain. Avoid hot water, which will set the stain.
- For red wine, soak a cloth napkin with white wine and apply to the stain area. Then dab the stain with cool water.
- Rub toothpaste—the white, pasty kind only—onto the stain to make it easier to clean later.
- If you spilled the wine on your date, apologize, offer to pay the dry cleaning bill, and immediately pour or order another glass of wine.

Lipstick Stain

- Apply a generous amount of petroleum jelly to the spot. Baby wipes or wet towelettes will also remove most of the stain. Dry clean as soon as possible.
- Use a scarf to camouflage the area, unless it is on your date's pants.

Ripped Stocking

- Use clear nail polish or a spritz of hairspray to keep the run from spreading.
- If the rip is at the toe, stretch the toe out further and tuck the excess fabric under your foot so that the rip cannot be seen.

- If the rip is down the front, twist your pantyhose to your inner thigh so that the tear is less visible. Be careful as you twist to avoid ripping it further. Or put the hose on backwards, as long as they are not seamed or embellished.
- As a last resort, remove the stockings and go bare-legged.

HOW TO TREAT A PIMPLE

1 Apply a warm compress.
Soak a hand towel in hot water, then hold it against
the pimple for a minute or more.

2 Apply a topical medication.
Use any over-the-counter benzoyl peroxide product.

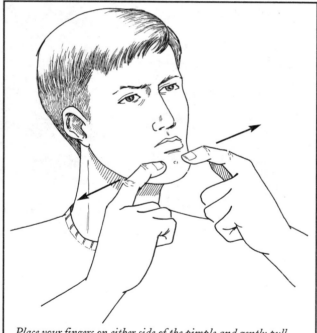

*Place your fingers on either side of the pimple and gently pull
away from the pimple. Do not push inward.*

3 Do not touch.
Leave the pimple alone for as long as possible.

4 Reassess the situation.
Immediately before your date, determine if the pimple has come to a head. If so, proceed to step 5.

5 Pop the pimple.
Place your fingers on either side of the pimple and gently pull away from the pimple. Do not push inward. The pimple will expel its contents if it is ready to, but no harm will be done if it is not.

6 Apply a cover-up.
Dab the now-empty pimple gently with a tissue to remove any remaining liquid. Apply any cosmetic with a green tint, which will conceal a pimple or the red mark left from a popped pimple (red and green are complementary colors and will negate each other).

HOW TO TREAT A SHAVING WOUND

Minor Cut

1 Rinse the cut with clean, cold water.

2 Apply alum salts or talcum powder.
Alum, a mineral sometimes sold as styptic powder or a styptic pencil, stops blood flow. Hold the alum in place for 10 to 20 seconds, depending on the severity of the wound. While effective, this technique can be painful, since it is literally applying "salt to the wound." The quickly dried cut may also form a noticeable scab. Alternatively, apply a liberal coating of talcum powder to the cut. Although slightly messier than alum, talcum is considerably less painful and will conceal the nicks and cuts.

If alum or talcum powder is not available, proceed to step 3.

3 Apply toilet paper.
Tear off a tiny piece of toilet paper or tissue and press it onto the cut for at least 15 seconds, until it adheres by itself.

4 Wait a few minutes.

5 Remove the toilet paper.
Moisten the paper before carefully pulling it from the cut. If it is not moistened, the paper may reopen the cut when you peel it off.

Major Laceration

Most serious shaving wounds occur to the neck, underneath the nose, or underneath an earlobe. The steps below focus on a neck laceration, but can apply to a major wound anywhere.

1 Apply firm pressure directly over the wound.
Place your fingertips at the point where the bleeding seems to be most severe.

2 If the bleeding stops, continue the pressure for an additional 10 minutes.
Remain still until the bleeding subsides. Then go to an emergency room.

3 If the bleeding does not stop, do not panic.
You probably have slowed the flow enough to have time for the next steps.

4 Pinch and hold the bleeding area.
Use your dominant thumb and index finger to pinch the skin where the blood flow is coming from. This will most likely close the vessel even if you cannot see it and will stop the serious bleeding.

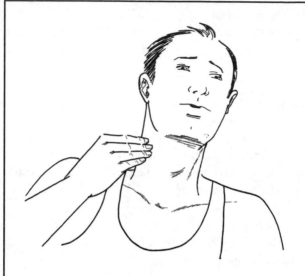

Apply firm pressure directly over the wound. Place your finger-tips at the point where the bleeding seems to be most severe.

Pushing above or below the site will help seal the area where blood vessels enter the wound.

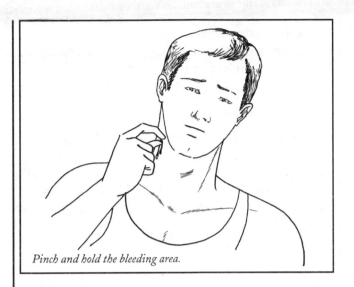

Pinch and hold the bleeding area.

5 Locate the bleeding vessel.

If the bleeding continues despite the steps above, use a piece of cloth or tissue to help you find the exact location of the cut vessel. Carefully ease off the finger pressure while wiping blood away from the wound with the cloth. This should make it easier to see the end of the cut vessel, or to pinpoint its location even if it is deep under the skin. When you see it, try pinching it again.

6 Apply pressure directly above and below the bleeding site.

If bleeding is still profuse, maintain finger pressure over the wound while pushing immediately above and below the bleeding site. This will seal the areas where blood vessels enter the wound.

7 Get to an emergency room.

If you are being driven to the emergency room, recline with your head raised slightly. Keep firm pressure on the wound even if the bleeding seems to slow.

Be Aware

- If the blood flows in a steady stream, you have hit a vein and can block the blood flow by pressing above the wound. If the blood is spurting, you have lacerated an artery and can block the blood flow by pressing (hard) below the wound. (See step 6.)

- There are four jugular veins. The external jugulars, paired on the right and left sides of the neck, are vulnerable because they lie right under the surface of the skin. The internal jugulars, also paired, lie close to the center of the neck front, but are about an inch under the skin in a protective sheath. If you accidentally cut your neck razor-shaving and notice a great deal of bleeding, you've probably cut the external jugular.

HOW TO DEAL WITH BODY ODOR

1 Apply cologne or perfume.
If you are on the way to a date and discover a problem with body odor, find a drugstore or department store. Apply the scent liberally.

2 Change your shirt or remove the offending article of clothing.
A simple change of clothing can often eliminate the odor, especially from an undershirt. Purchase a new shirt if you have to.

3 In mid-date, use one of the following techniques in the bathroom:
- Wet a stack of paper towels with hot water and a bit of soap. Take a second stack of towels and wet them without adding soap. Wash under your arms and wherever necessary with the soapy towels, then rinse with the remaining towels.
- Obtain chamomile tea bags from your server if you are in a restaurant. Soak them in hot water, then wipe down the offending areas with the bags. If possible, leave them in place for several minutes.
- Obtain a handful of fresh rosemary from the kitchen, wet it slightly, and rub it over the offending areas.
- Apply bathroom soap (powdered works best) to the offending areas to mask the scent.

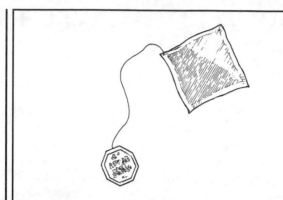

Soak chamomile teabags in hot water. Wipe the offending areas with the tea bags. If possible, leave the bags in place for several minutes.

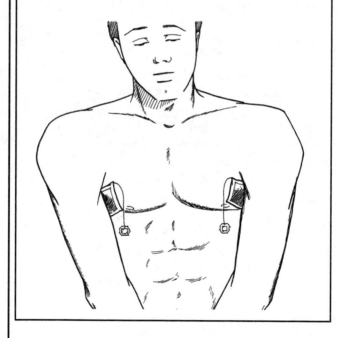

Be Aware

- To avoid B.O., try bathing using an antibacterial soap. Prolonged use can cause dryness, however.
- Avoid spicy or garlicky foods—these can cause body odor to worsen.
- Unusual body odor—not the typical "sweaty" smell—may indicate a more serious condition.
- Watch for the warning smells of B.O.:
    Beer smell may indicate a yeast infection.
    Nail polish smell may indicate diabetes.
    Ammonia smell may indicate liver disease.

how to deal with body odor

HOW TO DEAL WITH BAD BREATH

1 Chew gum or mints.
Excuse yourself from the table and head for the host's desk, where there may be a dish of mints. A waiter or busboy may also be able to give you a piece of gum. Go to the restroom and chew the gum for two minutes, then spit it out. This will get your saliva flowing and keep bad breath at bay for an hour or more. Chewing for more than a few minutes is not necessary. Sugar-free gum is best.

2 Chew parsley, mint, or a cinnamon stick.
On the way to the bathroom, pull your waiter aside and ask for one of these common garnishes. Parsley and fresh mint leaves are natural breath fresheners. A cinnamon stick, if chewed, will also clean your breath; do not use ground or powdered cinnamon. Most bartenders will have a stick on hand.

3 Order a salad or some fresh carrots.
If you cannot leave the table, order coarse foods that can help clean the tongue, a major source of bad breath.

Be Aware
Food odors are generally not as bad as you think, but when possible, avoid onions and garlic during your date.

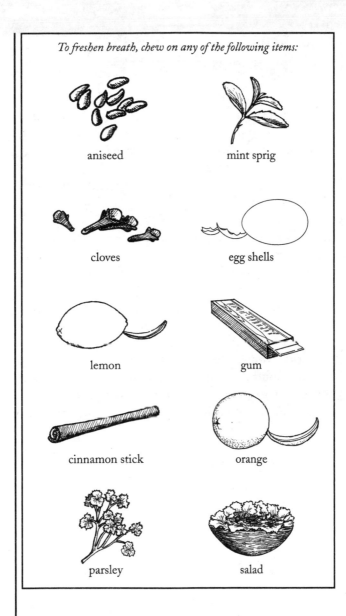

To freshen breath, chew on any of the following items:

aniseed

mint sprig

cloves

egg shells

lemon

gum

cinnamon stick

orange

parsley

salad

HOW TO PREVENT BAD BREATH

1 Floss.
Before going to bed, floss your teeth. Use unscented floss and smell it after each pass through. Areas that smell the worst need the most attention. Flossing may also help you live longer, as gum disease can shorten your life.

2 Sweep the tongue.
Gently sweep the mucus off the very back of your tongue with a commercially available tongue cleaner. Avoid cleaners made from sharp metal and do not scrape the tongue.

3 Brush with mouthwash.
Use an effective mouthwash. Shake if necessary, then pour some into the cap. Dip your toothbrush into it and brush your teeth properly for a few minutes. Do not use mouthwash and toothpaste at the same time as they can cancel out each other's active ingredients. Rinse and gargle with the rest of the mouthwash in the cap.

CHAPTER 3

RESTAURANT AND BAR SURVIVAL SKILLS

HOW TO GET
AN EMERGENCY
RESERVATION

BRIBE

1 Determine how much to offer the maitre d' as a bribe. The right amount will depend on the exclusivity and reputation of the establishment. Offer a minimum of $10. You usually get only one chance to try the bribe.

2 Fold the bill into your right palm.
Hold it between your thumb and forefinger.

3 Pass the bribe.
Shake his hand as you tell him how you are sure that he understands how important this night is to you. Be prepared, however, for the occasional maitre d' who takes your money and does not honor your request.

SOB STORY

1 Talk calmly to the maitre d'.
Controlled pleading can prove effective if you bend the right ear at the right time. A friendly, familiar demeanor is most likely to get the first available table. A whiny or arrogant voice will not help at all. If the maitre d' looks harried, wait until he or she has a moment to focus on you.

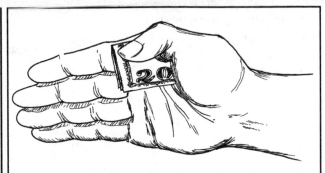

Hold the bill between your thumb and forefinger, then approach the maitre d' and shake his hand.

2 Explain your situation.
Be sure to stress the importance of the evening and the special need for a table, embellishing the facts as necessary: an anniversary dinner, a plan to propose marriage (but be prepared to produce a ring), a recovery from a long illness, an overdue reunion.

3 Speak with emotion.
Catch your voice, have difficulty breathing, shed a tear. You become harder to ignore. Also, the maitre d' will not want you upsetting the other waiting guests and creating a scene.

4 Appeal to the host's understanding nature.
Create the impression that you would be especially embarrassed in front of your date, since you told her you had a reservation.

how to get an emergency reservation

5 Look to fellow diners for sympathy.

If you cannot sway the host or maitre d', approach other diners and bribe or persuade them into giving up their table. Use the special event strategy (step 2, above). However, be careful to avoid offending the patrons or embarrassing your date. It is best to try this when your date leaves your side for a moment.

6 Pull rank.

Your final option is to play the "do you know who I am?" card. Unfortunately, you actually have to be somebody for this one to work.

Be Aware

- Do not try the "lost reservation" ploy; no one believes it anyway. Claiming that the restaurant is at fault for misplacing your reservation provokes confrontation rather than conciliation, and rarely results in a table.

- You can try the "celebrity name drop," but it could backfire. Asking for a table in the name of a celebrity will sometimes get you seated even though the celebrity is "late" in arriving, but the host may also ask you to wait until your group is all present before seating you—and you will be precluded from using other tactics.

HOW TO SAVE YOUR DATE FROM CHOKING

1 Speak firmly.

Keep your voice low and your sentences short. All communications should be in the imperative. Explain that you are going to perform the Heimlich maneuver.

2 Tell your date to stand up and stay put.

3 Hug your date from behind.

Put your arms around your date and make one hand into a fist.

4 Place your fist in your date's solar plexus.

The solar plexus is the first soft spot in the center of the body, between the navel and the ribs.

5 Place your other hand, palm open, over your fist.

6 Tell your date to bend forward slightly.

If your date does not respond, push on the upper back and repeat, "Lean forward."

7 Pull your fist in and up.

Use force and a quick motion. This will push out the residual lung gas under pressure, clearing any obstructions from the trachea.

8 | Repeat steps 3 through 7 several times if choking persists.

9 | After several unsuccessful attempts, instruct your date to bend over the back of a chair.
The top of the chair should be at the level of your date's hips.

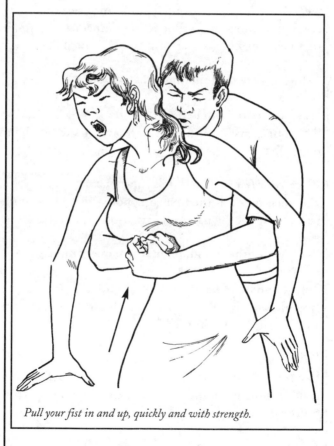

Pull your fist in and up, quickly and with strength.

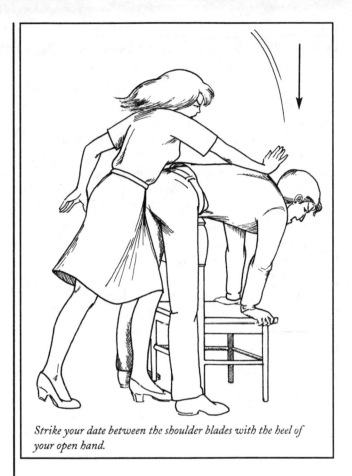

Strike your date between the shoulder blades with the heel of your open hand.

10 Strike your date between the shoulder blades with the heel of your open hand.

The blow generates gaseous pressure in a blocked airway and, with a head-down position, sometimes works when the Heimlich does not.

Be Aware

- If the choking is noiseless—or if your date raises her hands to her throat—then the air passage may be completely blocked and you must proceed quickly.
- If your date is coughing or gagging, you simply need to be polite, smile sympathetically, and offer water when the choking is over. Water does nothing for choking, but it gives the choker some time to regain dignity.
- In most cases, the first thrust of the Heimlich maneuver will dislodge the choked item from the trachea. Once the choking is over, your date will need some time to recover: a sip of brandy, a quiet moment. Do not rush your date to the emergency room; in most cases, there is no need to go to the hospital after the blockage has been removed.

HOW TO SURVIVE IF YOU HAVE EXCESSIVE GAS

1 Limit your lactose intake during the date.
Many people suffer from an inability to digest milk sugar, or lactose. Colon bacteria ferment the milk sugar, forming a gas that creates a bloated feeling. Keep your intake to less than half a cup at a sitting, and avoid dairy products before your date.

2 Eat a small meal.
Eating a huge dinner on a date is a sure-fire way to precipitate gas.

3 Avoid gas-forming foods.
Bacteria ferment the indigestible carbohydrates in beans, broccoli, cabbage, and other vegetables and fruits into gases.

4 Drink peppermint tea.
Replace an after-dinner drink with a cup or two of peppermint tea. This herb may give you some relief from the gas discomfort that follows a meal.

5 Emit the gas in private.
As a last resort, head to the bathroom. If you feel bloated but are unable to pass gas easily, you can facilitate the emission of gas as follows:

Kneel on the floor, bend forward, and stretch your arms out in front of you. Keep your buttocks high in the air, forming a triangle with your upper body and the floor.

Place paper towels on the floor. Kneel on the towels, bend forward to the floor, and stretch your arms out in front of you. Keep your buttocks high in the air, forming a triangle with your upper body and the floor. This position will force out the unwanted gas and relieve the pressure.

Be Aware

- On average, humans produce ¾ of a liter of gas daily, which is released 11 to 14 times a day.
- Men typically produce more gas than women because they consume more food.

GASSY FOODS TO AVOID

No two digestive systems are alike. Experiment with foods to determine which ones affect you most. In the meantime, exercise caution around the following high-risk items:

- Beans (particularly baked beans)
- Borscht
- Broccoli
- Brussels sprouts
- Cabbage
- Carbonated beverages
- Cauliflower
- Chili
- Cucumbers
- Fatty foods
- Fresh fruit
- Grains and fiber, especially pumpernickel bread
- Gum
- Onions
- Oysters
- Salads (green)

HOW TO SURVIVE IF YOUR CREDIT CARD IS DECLINED

TALK WITH THE MANAGER

1 **Be subtle.**

After the waiter informs you that your card has been declined, excuse yourself from the table and head for the reception desk. Explain the situation to the manager and show whatever identification you have. Ask him or her what you might do. Call the credit card company and inquire about your card. Speak firmly and sternly to the company. Ask the credit card company to extend your credit temporarily and immediately by the amount that you need.

2 **Offer collateral.**

Offer to leave something of value until you can return with the payment. Do not use your date as collateral. Offer a watch or a driver's license.

3 **Provide references.**

If you are known at any other restaurants, ask the manager to check with them, and say the management there will vouch for you. Promise to return immediately with payment.

4 | Seek funds.
Order another drink for your date (at the table or the bar) and confess the situation. Dash home for money or to a friend's house for a loan. Alternatively—unless it is the first date—you can ask your date to pay.

DINE AND DASH

1 | Accept the consequences.
You will never be able to be seen in this restaurant again if you skip out. Your date may be offended and embarrassed. And if this restaurant is in an area that you frequent, you may be identified and caught later.

2 | Tell your date the plan.
You do not want to catch your date off guard. Do not abandon your date, since she will likely be very upset and may help the authorities track you down. Plan to leave together.

3 | Plan your route of escape.
The best route is through the front door. However, restaurant staff may give chase. Assume that you will be followed. Visualize where you are going once you exit the restaurant. Head toward crowded or darkened areas.

4 | Wait until the staff is busy.
Have your belongings within reach for a hasty retreat. Do not appear anxious or ready to bolt.

5 Pretend to pay the bill with cash.

Place whatever bills you have in the bill holder with the check. The illusion of a cash payment will buy you valuable minutes of escape time; your waiter isn't likely to count the money until he reaches the nearest available cash register.

6 Walk confidently out the door.

Proceed slowly and with authority.

7 As soon as you are outside, run.

8 If you are being followed, do not go directly to your car.

It is very easy for your pursuer to jot down your license number. Wait at least twenty minutes before returning to your vehicle.

Be Aware

Stiffing the restaurant is illegal and may land you in jail, where the food is not very good. Arrange to pay the restaurant, directly or through a third party, as soon as you can. Include a message encouraging them to be more understanding of customers with credit card problems in the future.

Wash Dishes

1 Offer to wash dishes.

Tell the manager that you are willing to work to cover the cost of your meal. Explain that you have experience with the technology involved.

2 Prepare to get wet.

Take off your jacket, your watch, and any jewelry. (Men should also remove tie and long-sleeve shirt, if wearing an undershirt.) Take off your glasses (unless you have a major problem seeing without them). It is hot and wet in the kitchen. Ask for an apron, if available.

3 Prerinse the dirty dishware.

Remove the dirty dishes from the bus tub. Load the dishes into a square peg rack (a 20-by-20-inch plastic tray with holes in the bottom), place the peg rack over a slop sink, and rinse with a hose.

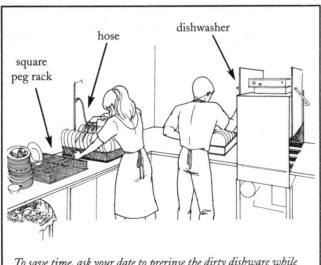

To save time, ask your date to prerinse the dirty dishware while you slide the loaded racks into the dishwasher.

4 Lift the door to the dishwasher and slide in the rack.

5 Close the dishwasher door and begin the wash cycle. Most machines begin automatically when locked, but you may need to press the start button. When the cycle is done, raise the door on the opposite side of the machine and remove the peg rack. Some systems utilize a conveyor belt that has claws to grab onto and pull the peg rack through the wash cycle.

6 Place the peg rack with the clean dishes in a drying rack.
The drying rack may be a wheeled racking system that holds many peg racks. Or it could be a slanted rack mounted on the wall. When the rack is placed on the angled wall unit, the excess water drips onto the stainless steel shelving. The dishes are now ready for use.

HOW TO FEND OFF COMPETITORS FOR YOUR DATE

1 Evaluate the situation.
Are you on a first date that is not going well? Is your date paying more attention to the interloper than to you? Do you want to continue dating this person?

2 Determine the seriousness of the offense.
Is it a passing rude drunk, a persistent boor, or someone seriously interested in leaving with your date? How big is the interloper? These factors will determine your response.

3 Stand your ground.
Put your arms around your date, whisper in her ear, and kiss and caress her. Show the suitor that your date is enamored with you, and you with her.

4 Place yourself in the "pickup screen" position.
Wedge yourself between the suitor and your date, with your back to the suitor. Try to block the suitor's path of vision. An "accidental" bump or push with your shoulders or buttocks may be appropriate.

Assume the "pickup screen" position by wedging yourself between the suitor and your date, with your back to the suitor. Try to block the suitor's path of vision.

5 | Ask the interloper to stop.
Politely but firmly explain that you are trying to have a conversation with your date and that you would both prefer to be left alone. If the suitor persists, use humor or sarcasm to diffuse the situation. Tell him you can offer him a few phone numbers, or tell him that tonight she's taken, but you will let him know when she's available.

6 | If the suitor is with friends, enlist their help to rein him in.

7 | Ask your date to tell the suitor to back off.
Your date should tell him that she's flattered but not interested.

8 | Try to leave.
If given the choice, choose flight over fight. Suggest to your date that you both move to a table or go to a new establishment. A fight generally doesn't make the evening go any better.

How to Treat a Black Eye

1 | Make a cold compress.
Put crushed ice in a plastic bag and wrap the bag in a thin piece of cloth. Alternatively, use a bag of frozen vegetables or a cold, raw steak.

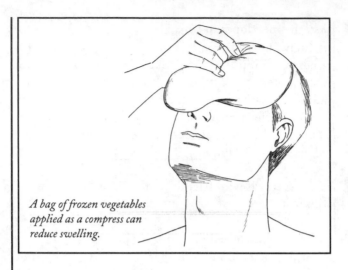

A bag of frozen vegetables applied as a compress can reduce swelling.

2 Sit down, tilt your head back, and cover your eye with the compress.

Use minimal pressure. This position allows gravity to aid in swelling reduction. If the compress is too cold to hold over your eye, use a thicker cloth. Keep the compress over your eye for an hour.

3 Take a painkiller.

For pain, take acetaminophen or ibuprofen.

How to Treat a Broken Nose

1 Stop the bleeding.

Tilt your head back slightly. Pinch the bridge of your nose (the region just below the hard cartilage) closed, not just the nostrils. Hold a tissue underneath your nostrils to catch the blood.

2 Apply a cold pack or ice immediately.
Keep your head tilted back. Continue to apply ice as needed to keep the swelling down.

3 Do not reset a broken nose yourself.
The only reason for you to attempt to relocate the position of the nose is if you are having trouble breathing through your mouth. If you aren't getting any air, you can attempt to adjust the position of your nose so that you can breathe through it, but this will be quite painful.

4 Seek medical attention.

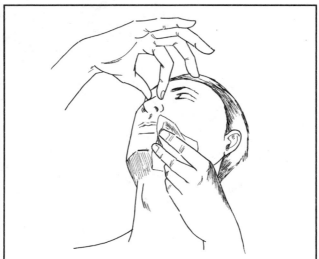

If your nose is broken, pinch the bridge of your nose (the region just below the hard cartilage) closed, not the nostrils. Hold a tissue underneath your nostrils to catch the blood.

Be Aware

The following symptoms indicate a more serious injury and the immediate need for professional care:

- Bleeding from the nose does not stop within 10 minutes
- Bleeding from both nostrils
- Trouble breathing through your nose
- Eye pain, trouble seeing, or blood on the surface of the eye
- Clear, watery fluid leaking out of the nose after the injury
- Swelling, bruising, or tenderness extending over the cheek area or below the eye

HOW TO DEAL WITH A DRUNKEN DATE

1 Avoid confrontation.
You realize your date is drunk, but he might not believe it. Keep the conversation light and happy, but don't let him have any more to drink. Suggest a change of plans, like a walk outside.

2 Keep your date on his feet.
Support him as needed. Put your arm around his waist, putting his arm over your shoulder. If that doesn't work, try holding him up by the belt. If you cannot hold your date upright, keep him seated and call a taxi.

3 Lead your date out into the air.
Bars are often smoky and short of oxygen, and oxygen is a major factor in reducing drunkenness. Calmly walk your date outside to get some fresh air into his lungs. This may help him become more awake and aware. If he objects, say you need to go outside to make a phone call.

4 Encourage your date to vomit.
If your date is so drunk that he cannot walk, or if he is speaking unintelligibly, he should expel alcohol from his system. Vomiting purges the stomach and prevents more alcohol from entering the bloodstream. Make sure your date rehydrates after purging. If your

Suggest a walk outside, to get some fresh air.

date falls to the floor and passes out, roll him onto his side to prevent him from choking on his vomit.

5 Watch for alcohol poisoning.
Signs of alcohol poisoning include tremors, unresponsiveness, unconsciousness, and lack of breathing.

If you suspect alcohol poisoning, position your date on his side, stay with him, and have someone call 911 for assistance.

6 Help your date to sober up.
See the next section, "How to Sober Up Fast."

Be Aware

- Common "cures" for drunkenness such as coffee or a cold shower are generally not effective; they will simply produce a more awake or wet drunk.
- Your body burns off approximately one drink an hour. It makes little difference if your drink is a 1-ounce shot of whiskey, a 5-ounce glass of wine, or a 12-ounce mug of beer—all contain similar amounts of alcohol. If you consume more than one drink per hour, you run the risk of becoming intoxicated. To minimize dehydration, drink a glass of water between rounds.
- If your drunk date goes to the restroom, stand outside and keep talking to him to be sure he remains conscious and responsive.

HOW TO SOBER UP FAST

1 Avoid pills.

Do not take ibuprofen, acetaminophen, or aspirin just before, during, or after drinking. Acetaminophen may cause liver damage in conjunction with alcohol. Ibuprofen can cause severe stomach irritation. Aspirin thins the blood, which may exacerbate a hangover.

2 Drink lots of fluids.

Dehydration from alcohol can be treated with water, sweet juices, or sports drinks. Orange juice and tomato juice contain potassium, which will help overcome the shaky feeling of a major hangover.

3 Take vitamins.

A good multivitamin or vitamin B complex combats vitamin depletion.

4 Eat.

Starchy foods—bread, crackers, rice, or pasta—break down into sugar, which speeds absorption of alcohol into your system. A spoonful of honey (which is high in fructose) helps to quickly burn off any remaining alcohol in the stomach. Listen to your body's cravings: if eggs sound good, eat them. If something spicy sounds better, eat that. There are no right or wrong things to eat; just take your food slowly and in small amounts.

5 Rest or sleep for as long as possible.

chapter 3: restaurant and bar survival skills

6 Repeat steps 2 through 5 if you wake up with a hangover.

HOW TO PREVENT A HANGOVER

- Eat before you begin to drink and snack while drinking.
- If you do not eat, coat your stomach with a full glass of milk.
- Pace yourself and drink water between drinks.
- Drink clear liquors. Some spirits are higher in congeners (impurities) than others; red wine, brandies (including cognac), and whiskies usually have more than other types of alcohol. Generally, the clearer your spirit, the fewer impurities and the less severe the hangover.
- Champagne and mixed drinks made with carbonated sodas allow for faster alcohol absorption; they should be sipped slowly.
- Know your limits. In most states, a Blood Alcohol Content (B.A.C.) of .10 means you are legally drunk—and some states now use the stricter .08 B.A.C. For most average-size adults, this can mean as few as two drinks in an hour.
- Do not mix your liquors. Each spirit has different toxins that must be processed by your liver. It is best not to overload it.
- Before going to bed, have a snack of a banana or cheese and crackers.
- Keep water beside your bed and drink it if you awaken during the night.

HOW TO
CARRY A DATE
WHO IS PASSED OUT

1 Plan to carry your date only for a short distance.
Your destination should be a nearby couch, taxi, or bed. Do not attempt to carry him a long way.

2 Prepare to lift.
Bend your knees and place your stronger arm under your date's back and the other under his knees. Your arms should go all the way under and across his body.

3 Begin to lift your date.
Use the strength of your legs and knees, holding them close to your body and keeping your back straight. Do not lift with your back.

4 Stand up quickly.
In one continuous motion, rotate your date's body so that your stronger arm guides him over your opposite shoulder. The motion should be like tossing a sack of potatoes. His upper body should be hanging over your back, his lower body hanging over your front. Steady him with your other hand.

5 Walk to your destination.

chapter 3: restaurant and bar survival skills

Place your stronger arm under your date's back.

Keep your back straight and lift with your knees.

Rotate your date's body over your opposite shoulder. The motion should be like tossing a sack of potatoes.

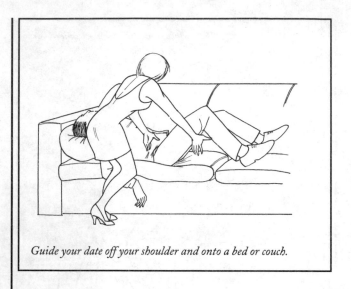

Guide your date off your shoulder and onto a bed or couch.

6 Lower your date.
Bending your knees and keeping your back straight, guide your date off your shoulder and onto a bed or couch or into a chair.

HOW TO SURVIVE IF YOU ARE STOPPED BY THE POLICE

1 Pull over immediately.

Put your hazard lights on, take off your sunglasses, turn off the radio, and turn off the engine. Roll down your window. Keep your hands in plain sight, preferably on the steering wheel. Make sure your date's hands are also in view.

Address the officer as "Officer." Respect for authority will get you out of the situation much more quickly and easily.

2 | Address the officer as "Officer."
Displaying proper respect will get you out of the situation much more quickly and easily.

3 | Always tell the truth about your record.
The police officer already knows (or will soon know) the answers to the questions asked. Do not claim that you have a clean driving record if this is not the case.

4 | Do not argue with or challenge the officer.
Not only will you look foolish and/or arrogant in front of your date, your comments may be recorded on the officer's copy of the ticket so they can be used to refresh the officer's memory in court. Do not give the officer a reason to take a personal interest in you or your case, which would only encourage the officer to show up in court if you decide to fight the ticket. (Many defendants succeed in court because the officer is not present to testify.)

5 | Do not falsely claim your innocence.
The officer has seen you do it, and denying the infraction or making lame excuses will only serve to irritate the officer.

6 | Use the presence of your date to help you.
Try saying, "Officer, I'm sorry. I'm on a date and I guess I was pretty distracted. I'm a bit nervous and probably was paying more attention to her than to my driving. I'll be more careful." This may appeal to the officer's sense of romance, helping you get off completely.

If You Are Arrested

1 | Contact a bail bondsman.

A bondsman will need to know the name of the jail you are in, the charges against you, the amount of your bail, and your booking number. The bondsman will charge you a fee of about 10 percent of your total bail amount and then make a guarantee to the court on your behalf that you will show up for your court date. (If bail is set at $50,000, for example, you will be required to pay the bondsman a nonrefundable fee of approximately $5,000.)

2 | Be prepared to put up collateral.

When a bondsman writes a bail bond for you, he is on the hook for the entire amount of your bail should you not show up in court. He will demand a guarantee that you can pay him the full amount if you should jump bail. Ninety percent of the time, large bail bonds are secured with real property. Evaluate your assets in light of the amount of bail.

CHAPTER 4
BEDROOM
SURVIVAL SKILLS

HOW TO DEAL WITH A BAD KISSER

Too Aggressive

1 Slow him down.
Ask your date to kiss more gently. Say, "Can I show you the way I really like to kiss?" and slowly lean forward to offer a demonstration.

2 Kiss your date.

3 Draw away from the kiss.
Briefly drawing away from the kiss is another way of saying slow down.

4 Gently hold his face.
Your hands can provide a caress, and also prevent him from zooming back in for more.

5 Tilt his head.
While your hands are in place, tilt his head to the angle of greatest comfort. Tilt your head accordingly.

6 Surround his mouth with gentler kisses.
Reinforce the message by sighing and saying, "I love it like this."

7 Repeat as necessary.

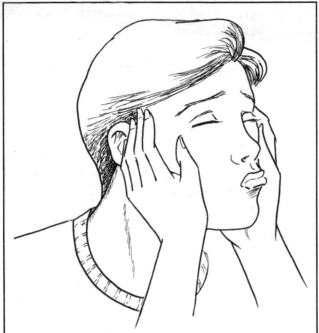

Tilt his head to the angle of greatest comfort, then adjust your position accordingly. Use your hands to hold him back or draw him in.

Be Aware

Very aggressive tongue kissing may be just right when you are very aroused, but not so great when you are just beginning. Be careful not to scare him away from things you might enjoy later.

how to deal with a bad kisser

Too Passive

1 Look your date in the eye.
A warm, smiling gaze signals affection and also lets him know something is about to happen.

2 Hold his face.

3 Kiss him passionately.
The kiss should be as deep and passionate as you want his to be. Remember to tilt your date's head before kissing him.

4 Break away from the kiss.
Murmur, "Mmm, kiss me back harder." You are taking charge of the situation.

5 Pause and redirect.
If you are still not getting the desired result—if his tongue is not responding—shift to lip-focused rather than deep-mouth kissing.

Be Aware
You may be dealing with someone who thinks your kissing style is too aggressive. He may be passively resisting your technique instead of trying to slow you down by using the more direct response to "too aggressive" kissing (see above).

Too Wet

1 Keep your kisses focused on the lips.
Do not venture inside the mouth.

2 Use your thumbs to wipe away excess wetness.
Gently outline his lips with a thumb or other finger.
This will serve as a sensual caress and will also remove
excess moisture.

How to Deliver the Perfect Kiss

1 Cradle your date's face with your hands.
Look into his eyes.

2 Tilt his head.

3 Tilt your head.

4 Bring your mouth toward his mouth.
Gradually move closer.

5 Gently touch your lips to his.
Focus initially on the lips, giving soft, quick kisses.
Slowly part your lips, letting your tongue softly dart
out to touch his lips. This is an excellent way to gauge
your partner's receptiveness to furthering the kiss. If
lips part, proceed to the next level.

6 | Explore delicately with your tongue.
Open your mouth wider and push your tongue into his mouth. Probe the various parts of his mouth. Run your tongue over the teeth. Imagine your tongue fencing with your partner's tongue, lunging, darting, and parrying.

7 | Take frequent breaks.
Keeping your tongues inside each other's mouths for an extended period of time will produce a very sloppy, wet kiss. Move your head away from his every so often. This will also allow you to catch your breath.

8 | Know when to stop.
End the kiss before your jaw begins to ache, or before you are both worn out. It may be time to move on to other activities, or it may be fine to stop and leave him wanting more.

Be Aware
If either or both of you wear glasses, remove them prior to a prolonged kissing session. Wearing glasses for a medium-intensity, brief kiss is acceptable, but glasses may hinder greater intimacy (and they may get fogged up or even scratched). Set them someplace safe, where you will not be likely to roll onto them later.

HOW TO REMOVE DIFFICULT CLOTHING

BACK-CLASPING BRA (WITH ONE HAND)

1 Move your date forward.
If your date is lying on her back or leaning against a sofa, you will not have the necessary space to attempt this maneuver. Use a gentle embrace to guide her into a position so that you have access to her back.

2 Visualize the clasp.
Most bras have a hook-and-eye closure. The hooks are generally on her right side; the eyes will be on her left side.

3 Reach your right hand around to the clasp.
Bend your index finger over the bra clasp and place it between the fabric and her skin.

4 Brace your thumb against the eyes of the clasp.

5 Holding your index finger down, push the hook-side of the bra with your thumb.
It may take a few attempts before you get good at this, so do not be discouraged—try again.

6 Slide the now-open bra off her arms.

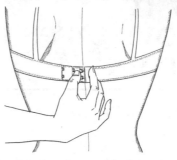

Brace your thumb against the eyes of the clasp.

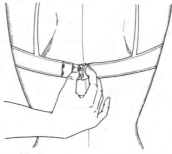

Holding your index finger down, push the hookside of the bra with your thumb.

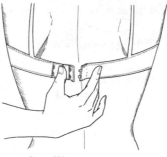

Slide the now-open bra off her arms.

Be Aware

The bigger the breasts, the bigger the challenge, since the closure on her bra is bearing more weight and is likely to be more taut.

FRONT-CLASPING BRA

1 Determine the type of clasp.

There are two different varieties: a pin-in-slot clasp, which has a pin inserted vertically in a slot, and a clicker clasp. Clicker clasps, when closed, often look like a circle or an oval.

2 For a pin-in-slot clasp, pull the pin upward.

This will free the two cups, and you can proceed to step 4.

3 For a clicker clasp, push both ends away from you.

Place your thumbs at the center of the clasp and, using a motion similar to snapping a small wafer in half, apply pressure until it unclicks. Then lift up and separate the two halves of the closure. Depending on the clasp, you will need to raise either the left side or the right side first; try it one way, then the other.

4 Slide the now-open bra off her arms.

Be Aware

To maximize intimacy, maintain eye contact throughout the entire process. Do not look away unless you need to take a quick glance at the closure.

TIGHT BOOTS

1 **Sprinkle powder down the shaft of each boot.**
Talcum powder or baking powder will reduce the sweat and humidity inside the boots, making them easier to remove.

2 **Position your date on the edge of a bed or couch.**

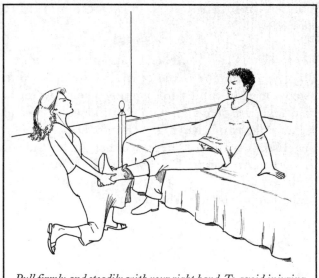

Pull firmly and steadily with your right hand. To avoid injuring the wearer, do not jerk the boot.

3 Position yourself opposite your date.
Sit in a chair braced against a wall, or rest one knee on the floor with the other foot flat on the floor.

4 Cup the heel of the boot in your right hand.
Place your left hand on the area of the boot that covers the front of the leg/shin. Instruct your date to relax the foot in the boot.

5 Pull firmly and steadily with your right hand.
You should feel some give in the heel. When you cannot move the boot anymore, gently rock the boot back and forth. Your date should point the foot only slightly. To avoid injuring the wearer, do not jerk the boot.

6 Slide the boot off slowly.
Caress the newly released foot.

HOW TO FAKE
AN ORGASM

1 **Begin your vocal and physical ascent.**
During sexual activity, start to make noise and move rhythmically.

2 **Moan and cry out, building in volume and intensity.**
You may say your partner's name over and over. Many people, in the thralls of ecstasy, will blurt out sentences or requests that are utterly incomprehensible: try this occasionally.

3 **Move faster rhythmically and then increasingly "out of control."**
As you approach "climax," increase the tempo of your movements, particularly of the hips. Add jerky movements. If you have not moved or vocalized much before you start to fake the orgasm, it will seem all the more fake, so you might need to fake enjoyment all the way through. (Note: If you do not usually move your hips during sex, try it. You may find it affects your arousal enough that you will need less faking.)

4 **Contract your muscles.**
For many people, this is an involuntary side effect of an orgasm; the classic examples are toe-curling or fingers clutching the sheets. You might also arch your back, scrunch your facial muscles, or open your mouth wide.

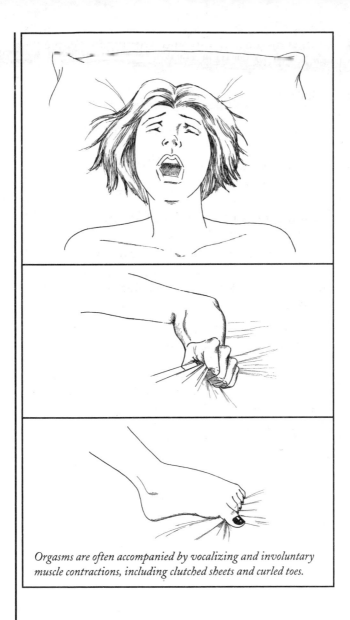

Orgasms are often accompanied by vocalizing and involuntary muscle contractions, including clutched sheets and curled toes.

5 Ratchet up the moaning and writhing in volume and intensity.

6 Culminate in a loud moan or cry.

7 Slow down immediately, tensing your body.

8 Relax, as if exhausted or spent.
Smile with enjoyment.

How to Detect a Real Orgasm

Real orgasms are not always as theatrical and loud as fake ones. Some people are silent comers and do not exhibit many visible signs. Real orgasms tend to have some or all of the following elements:
- Changes in breathing
- Increased vocalizations
- Intensified movements
- Involuntary muscle contractions
- A pink or reddish flush on the face and chest
- Sweat on the shoulders
- Pelvic muscle contractions

Be Aware

- Be sure that you want to fake the orgasm. You will be sending your partner a message that you are enjoying the sex more than you really are. If your partner is an ongoing lover or spouse, think hard before giving him or her the impression that he or she is doing everything right when that is not the case. If you are enjoying a one-night encounter, consider why it should make a difference to you if your partner thinks you have had an orgasm or not.

- Men can fake orgasms too, particularly if a condom is being used.

- Do not accuse your partner of faking an orgasm if they are not demonstrative, spasmodic, and loud. Conversely, do not accuse your partner of faking if they display all the characteristics of a faked orgasm.

HOW TO CREATE PRIVACY IF YOUR DOOR DOES NOT LOCK

BLOCKADE A DOOR THAT OPENS INWARD

1 Find a straight-backed wooden or metal chair.

2 Shut the door.

3 Place the chair about a foot from the door.
How far away you place it will depend upon how tall the chair's back is, so adjust the distance accordingly.

4 Tilt the chair backward so that the top of the chair is wedged underneath the doorknob.
The seat should be facing upward. If necessary, pull the bottom of the chair out a bit so that the top of the chair will fit under the knob.

5 Push down on the front of the seat or the bottom of the front legs.
When the chair is securely wedged, kick it in further to make the blockade tight.

6 Place a large item of furniture (a trunk or dresser) directly against the chair.
The chair buttressed by other furniture will make it extremely difficult to open the door from outside.

Tilt the chair backward so that the top of the chair is wedged underneath the doorknob.

BLOCKADE A DOOR THAT OPENS OUTWARD

Using a rope, fishing line, phone cord, or electrical cord, tie the doorknob to the leg of a heavy dresser or other immovable object. Loop the rope around the knob several times so that it will not slip off, and be sure the line to the fixture remains taut. Anyone trying to enter the room will be unable to pull the door open.

Entry Alarm

1 Collect stackable items that will make a noise if toppled.
Empty cans—between 6 and 10—work best. Jars or bottles will also work in an emergency, but the glass might break.

2 Select a door.
Alarm a door other than the one to the room you are in, so that you will have advance warning if someone is coming. For example, alarm the front door if you are in the bedroom.

3 Shut the door.

4 Stack the items against the door.

5 Retreat to your room.
If someone opens the alarmed door, the items will topple and you will have time to prepare for their approach.

Alternate Method
Tie several cans, cowbells, or Christmas ornaments to the doorknob. When your intruder opens the door, the objects will knock against each other, warning you of an interruption.

HOW TO HAVE SEX IN A SMALL SPACE

AIRPLANE LAVATORY

1 Pick a rendezvous time.
Select a time when you are least likely to have to wait in line and when you will not be disturbed. The best times are just before the plane reaches cruising altitude or during the in-flight entertainment.

2 As the plane is ascending, listen for a beep from the in-flight messaging system.
The first beep comes without a subsequent announcement and indicates to the flight attendants that cruising altitude has almost been reached and that it is safe to begin their preparations. The FASTEN YOUR SEATBELT sign will still be illuminated, but the flight attendants will get up. As soon as the flight attendants clear the aisle, head for the lavatory. Try to select one that is not visible from the galleys. Have your date wait at least a minute, then meet you in the lavatory. You should hear the beverage carts roll by. After a few minutes, the flight attendants will begin to serve drinks, blocking the aisle from passenger access. Alternatively, or in addition, proceed to step 3.

3 Meet during the movie.
Plan your rendezvous for the beginning of the film, preferably when the film is at least fifteen minutes

underway. Most passengers and flight attendants stay out of the aisles and galley areas during the entertainment portion of the flight, so you will have more privacy. You should proceed to the lavatory first, to be followed a minute later by your date.

4 | Put down the toilet seat lid and clean it.
Wipe the seat with sani-wipes if they are available, or use a wet paper towel with soap. Place paper towels or a sanitary toilet seat cover on top for extra protection.

5 | Be quiet and be quick.
You will not have a lot of time before people are lining up to get into the restroom.

6 | Be ready for turbulence.
The safest positions involve one partner sitting on the closed toilet seat. Then, in the event of bumpy air, neither partner will be too close to the ceiling, risking a concussion.

7 | If you do encounter turbulence, hold on.
Brace yourself against the sink and do not try to stand up or move. Stay where you are and ride it out.

8 | Exit the lavatory together, feigning illness.
It is illegal to have sex in an airplane bathroom—so deny it in the unlikely event that you are asked. Tell the flight attendant or other passengers that one of you was ill and the other was offering assistance.

ELEVATOR

1 Find a building with an older elevator.

Many older elevators have an emergency STOP button that will allow you to halt the elevator. On other units, flipping the switch from RUN to STOP will cause an alarm bell to sound. You will still have plenty of time, at least ten or fifteen minutes, possibly as long as an hour, before firefighters or other emergency personnel are able to access the elevator cabin.

2 Alternatively, look for a freight elevator with padding on the walls.

Freight elevators will be less likely to have an alarm that sounds when the STOP switch is thrown. The padding may also muffle sound and provide comfort.

3 Look for a camera.

Virtually all new elevators have security cameras, as do some older ones, including freight elevators. If a camera is present, cover the camera lens—it will probably be in a rear corner—with a piece of tape or with several postage stamps. The security system may include audio as well, however.

4 Stop the elevator between floors.

Elevator doors house a mechanical clutch that opens the corridor (outer) doors. If the elevator is not level with a floor, the corridor doors cannot open, and someone from the outside will not easily be able to open the inner doors.

5   Release the STOP button or flip the switch to RUN when you are ready to leave.

Exit the elevator normally. If emergency personnel are present, tell them there was a malfunction but that you are okay.

Be Aware

If the elevator is stopped level with a floor, an elevator technician will be able to open both the outer (corridor) doors and the inner (elevator) doors from the outside.

DRESSING ROOM

1   Look for a dressing room that has a door and walls that extend to the floor.

If all the dressing rooms have a gap between the floor and the walls, look for one with a secure door, rather than a curtain. If you are in a store that has several dressing rooms, look for the least-trafficked or least-monitored areas. Some dressing rooms have very hard-to-detect security systems—including two-way mirrors—so you cannot guarantee that you will not be seen.

2   Carry clothes as if you are going to try them on.

Trail after a demanding customer who is requiring the attentions of the sales associate on duty. When the employee is occupied, make your move and duck into the dressing room.

3 Have your partner follow behind a few minutes later.

4 Be quiet.
The walls to dressing rooms are thin.

5 Be quick.
Speed is important, especially if your legs are visible beneath the walls.

6 Depart from the dressing room one person at a time. Check your appearance in the mirror, and leave the store's clothes in the dressing room. If you are in the women's section of a department store, the woman should leave first and make sure the coast is clear. If you are in the men's department, the man should leave first.

Be Aware
For speed and efficiency in airplanes, elevators, and dressing rooms, be sure to wear loose, baggy clothing. Do not wear underwear.

HOW TO SURVIVE SNORING

1 Keep your date on her side or stomach.

Sleeping on the back tends to lead to snoring. If your date falls asleep on her back, change her position using one of the following techniques:

- The Pillow Lift: Grab the nearest corner of the pillow (the corner she is facing, if she is on her side) and lift it up until she begins to rustle and turn over. This may cause her to wake up momentarily and stop snoring.
- The Bed Flop: Actively flip yourself over (from one side to the other, or from your stomach to your back) with an unusually aggressive flop. Make it forceful enough to shake the bed. Often this will disturb her just enough to cause her to turn over as well.

2 Wake up your date.

If the more subtle approaches do not work, become more aggressive. A strategically placed elbow nudge or kick may awaken your date. Repeat until effective.

3 Use earplugs.

Be prepared for the worst—have earplugs handy. If you do not have earplugs, try using a small amount of wadded-up cotton from a cotton ball, or even toilet paper. Your final alternative is to sleep in separate rooms. It may not be romantic, but it is an effective temporary solution.

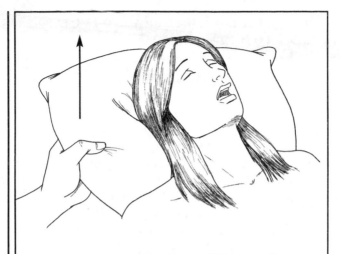

Grab the nearest corner of the pillow and lift it up until your date begins to rustle and turn over.

Be Aware

- Drinking alcohol promotes snoring, so prevent your date from drinking too much. Alcohol depresses the activity of nerves in the nasal air passages, enervating the airway muscles that would keep the air passages open at night and prevent snoring.
- Drinking coffee reduces snoring. Caffeine may stimulate the airway nerves, keeping them open. Caffeine may also make a person sleep more lightly, which can reduce snoring.

How to Find a Partner Who Is Less Likely to Snore

- Avoid the obese, as they have a higher incidence of snoring.
- Avoid individuals with short, fat necks, as these people also have a higher incidence of snoring.
- Avoid individuals who are constantly sniffing and snorting; this may indicate a chronic sinus condition that can cause snoring.
- Avoid heavy drinkers; high alcohol intake leads to a higher incidence of snoring.
- Avoid someone who consistently falls asleep in social situations. Tiredness may be a sign that this person is experiencing reduced quality of sleep due to a sleep disorder that may include snoring.

chapter 4: bedroom survival skills

HOW TO SURVIVE IF YOU WAKE UP NEXT TO SOMEONE WHOSE NAME YOU DON'T REMEMBER

AT THEIR PLACE

1 Do not panic.
Evidence of your partner's name exists somewhere nearby. Your task will be to find it before she awakens, or before she starts any sort of meaningful conversation.

2 Get up and go to the bathroom.
The bathroom is a normal place to visit first thing in the morning, and it is also a place where you might discover her name.

3 Look through the medicine cabinet for prescription medicines with her name on the label.

4 Sort through magazines, looking for subscription labels with her name and address.

5 Go through a wastebasket to find discarded junk mail addressed to her.

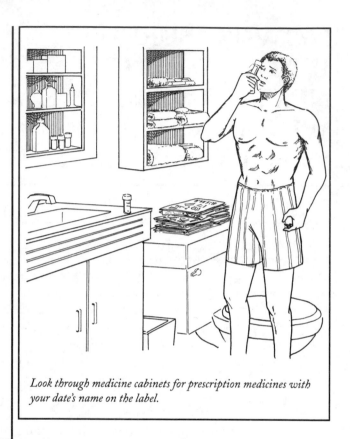

Look through medicine cabinets for prescription medicines with your date's name on the label.

6 Return to the bedroom.

If she is awake, ask her to make coffee for you. Use the time alone to search the bedroom for evidence. Look for: wallet, checkbook, ID or name bracelet, photo album, scrapbook, business cards (a stack of cards, not just one), or luggage labels. If she is sleeping, look for these and other items throughout the house.

Be Aware
Try to find at least two items with the same name to be certain that you have identified her, unless the name on one item rings a bell.

AT YOUR PLACE

1 Use terms of endearment when addressing her.
Do not guess at her name. Acceptable terms of endearment are:
- Honey/Sweetie/Cutie
- Darling/Baby/Sugar
- Beautiful/Handsome/Gorgeous

2 Unless you are certain you have ample time, do not go through her belongings.
If your partner is showering, you can count on having at least a few minutes of privacy to search through her belongings. Otherwise, do not risk it—it would be far more embarrassing to be caught searching through her possessions than to admit you cannot remember her name. (She may be in the same predicament.)

3 Ask leading questions while making small talk.
Fishing for information is risky and can backfire by calling attention to what you are trying to do. However, if you feel you can pull it off, try to trick her into revealing her name:
- While getting dressed, pull out your own ID and ask her if she thinks that your hair is better now or in the picture. Laugh about how silly you used

how to survive if you wake up next to someone whose name you don't remember

to look. Ask her if she likes the picture on her license. (She may think that you are checking her age.)

- Ask her if she ever had a nickname. She might say, "No, just [*Name*]."
- Ask her how she got her name.

4 As she is leaving, give her your business card and ask for hers.

If she does not have a business card, ask her to write her vital information on yours. Tell her you may want to send her a little surprise. Do not forget to send something later in the week and make sure that you spell her name correctly.

CHAPTER 5

RELATIONSHIP SURVIVAL

HOW TO SURVIVE IF YOU RUN INTO YOUR EX

Running into your ex at a party can be problematic for many reasons: lingering affection, pain over being dumped, unresolved emotions, passionate memories, or poor selection of your current date.

1 **Do not avert your gaze.**
Look him in the eye and smile. Shying away from eye contact only diminishes your power. Keep someone's gaze and you keep control.

2 Be nice.

3 **Do not sit.**
Do not let yourself get stuck in a corner or on a couch with your ex. Remain standing and be ready to move.

4 **Take charge of the conversation.**
Start by mentioning something that you noticed earlier in the day. This keeps the dialogue fresh and superficial and in your control, and helps you to avoid complimenting or talking about the ex. Be upbeat—enthusiasm is a handy tool. Breezing by someone indicates you are not fazed or upset.

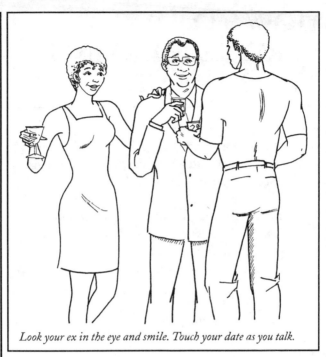

Look your ex in the eye and smile. Touch your date as you talk.

5 Introduce your date and send clear signals that this is who you are with now.

Touch your date as you converse with your ex, making it clear that you have moved on.

6 Keep your conversation short and sweet.

Tell your ex that you are "meeting friends," but that it was nice to see him. Or, tug your date's arm and say, "Oh look, there's Sally. I want you to meet her."

7 Move on.

HOW TO SURVIVE MEETING THE PARENTS

1 | Pay attention to your surroundings.
If you are prone to spilling things or tripping over rugs, move slowly and carefully. Present an image of confidence and poise.

2 | Greet them with a firm, but brief, handshake.
A weak handshake is a turnoff, but so is squeezing too hard. Shake hands so that the entire hand is clasped. Let go of the hand after a few pumps. Maintain eye contact.

3 | Do not kiss or hug the parents unless they make the first move.
If they offer air kisses, fine, but never kiss a potential in-law on the mouth. If they opt to hug you, do not retreat from it.

4 | Call them "Mr." and "Mrs." unless they ask you to address them by their first names.
This shows respect. Do not shorten or change their names or call them "Mom" or "Dad."

5 | Give them personal space.
Allow at least three feet of airspace during conversation.

Eye contact

Smile

Good posture

Firm handshake

Gift

At least three feet of personal space

6 Show poise.

Be positive, good natured, and relaxed. Smile, but not continuously: if you look happy all of the time, something's not right. Remember that good posture projects confidence and successfulness. Walk, stand, and sit up straight. Speak loud enough to be heard.

7 | Be sincere and be yourself.
Do not pretend to be someone you are not. People can spot a fake a mile away. Do not try too hard to make an impression. At the same time, do not act too familiar—no winking, shoulder punching, or joking. Follow their lead.

8 | Send a note or card the next day.
Mention how nice it was to finally meet them and that you look forward to seeing them again. If you stayed at their house for a while, thank them for an enjoyable visit.

Be Aware
Practicing the following social graces can help make a favorable impression:
- Ring the doorbell once only. Do not lean on the bell or pound the door.
- Turn off your cell phone and pager.
- If invited to dinner, bring wine, flowers, or dessert, even if they say not to.
- Wait to be invited inside, and wait to be seated. Do not sit down before they do.
- Pet the dog or cat.
- Compliment them on only one or two things: the view, the couch, a painting, the flowers—don't overdo it.
- Do not spend too much time in the bathroom (and do not go too often).

HOW TO SURVIVE IF YOU FORGET A BIRTHDAY

1 | Apologize. Apologize. Apologize.
Your apology might have to take several forms—flowers, verbal protestations, love letters, a special dinner. Be creative.

2 | Accept responsibility for your error.
Recognize sincerely that you blew it. Excuses will only make things worse.

3 | Acknowledge your partner's feelings.
Accept your partner's anger as valid and do not question or challenge any reaction. Say, "I can only begin to imagine how you must feel."

4 | Plan a special event to fix the mistake.
A weekend getaway, a night at a fancy hotel, or an extremely thoughtful gift will be necessary. However, do not show up two days late with a windfall of gifts, expecting that all will be forgiven. All the presents in the world cannot eliminate the need for talking the matter through.

HOW TO DEAL WITH A CHEATING LOVER

1 | Ask her outright.
If you suspect your lover is cheating on you, do not worry about embarrassment or gathering too much evidence. The fact that you are unsure of her fidelity is enough to raise the issue. If she expresses surprise by the question or hesitates, present your reasons for asking in as calm a way as possible.

2 | Do not act impulsively and end the relationship.
If you ascertain that she is cheating on you, all is not lost. Talk or cry together, and then spend some time apart. If this is the first time, seek counseling with your partner. Discuss why it happened and what it means to both of you. This could lead the two of you to be more honest, and perhaps more trusting and intimate.

3 | Discuss the seriousness of the affair.
Talk about whether the indiscretion was a one-time incident with someone of little consequence, or whether your partner is in an ongoing relationship. Talk about the difference and think hard about what the circumstances mean to both of you. Professional counseling can help clarify your feelings and priorities. It can also help you to rebuild a trusting relationship, if this is still desired.

4 Decide what you want first—then ask your partner to decide what she wants.

The best possibility is if you both want the same thing, either an end to your relationship or an end to the affair.

5 Act according to your wishes, not your partner's.

If you want to work it out but your partner does not, work on the relationship until you are certain you have tried your best to salvage things. If this is a recurring problem with your partner and you have talked about it at length before, it probably means that she wants out, or that you can expect her to continue having affairs. To end the relationship, go to page 150.

HOW TO HAVE AN AFFAIR AND NOT GET CAUGHT

1 Assemble an array of convincing alibis and witnesses to explain your frequent disappearances.
Telling your partner "I have to work late" will only get you so far. Enlist the help of a friend or colleague, and have them "invite" you to a reception or sports event, or call with an "emergency." Create a false trail of evidence by having them leave messages on your answering machine that your partner will hear.

2 Do not make multiple, obvious changes to your lifestyle.
Do not alter the way you dress or the foods you eat all at once. This will tip off your partner that something has changed.

3 Do not discuss topics you previously knew nothing about.
If your lover has encouraged you to become interested in sports or cooking or opera or other topics you never cared about, do not suddenly start talking about them with your partner, who may wonder—or ask—how you knew that.

Always pay cash. Avoid credit cards.

Use cell phones. Never use the hotel phone.

Use room service. Avoid popular restaurants.

Always drive separately. Never drive together.

how to have an affair and not get caught

4 | Do not change all your sexual habits at once.
An affair might make you more sexually adventurous, but do not try too many new things at once with your partner.

5 | Never leave for work wearing one outfit and return wearing another.
Keep a change of clothing in your car or at your office and wear that outfit with your lover. Afterward, change back into the clothing you wore when you left home. This will help avoid evidence of your indiscretion (e.g., lipstick, cologne or perfume, or inappropriate wrinkles). Make sure that you do the laundry that contains your "affair" clothing.

6 | Take a shower to remove the scent of the affair.
Bathing is especially necessary if you have been in a smoky bar, if your lover wears strong aftershave or perfume, or if you have a dog waiting at home.

7 | Never call your partner from a hotel or motel phone, or from a restaurant.
Use your cell phone only—caller ID may reveal your whereabouts.

8 | Pay bills in cash only.
Never use a credit card to charge meals, hotels, or day trips. Your partner will probably notice the increase in spending or find the charge slip. Make sure you have enough cash before you head off to your rendezvous; cash machine usage is traceable as well.

9 | **Drive in a separate car from your lover.**
Should there be an accident or a police incident, there will not be any official record of another passenger in the car with you. There will also be no unintentional physical traces—adjusted seat, forgotten scarf—of the passenger.

10 | **Do not go to fancy or popular restaurants with your lover.**
Out-of-the-way places are best; you are less likely to be spotted by friends of your partner. Places just out of town are even better. Room service in a hotel is very private.

IF YOU ARE CAUGHT

1 | **Do not deny your guilt.**
Admit your indiscretion immediately. Dissembling only makes matters worse.

2 | **Decide immediately whether or not you want to continue the affair.**
You will have to be clear about your choice. Ask yourself if you would rather continue with the lover or with your partner. Be honest with yourself and act accordingly.

3 | **If you want out of your relationship, cut the cord immediately and be ruthless.**
Do not try to be nice or understanding—it will only make things more difficult for your soon-to-be-ex-partner. Be a jerk—it will make it easier for them to

move on. Explain that you have simply fallen for someone else, that you can't help it, and that you realize that
your relationship must end.

4 | **If you want to continue your relationship, be prepared
to work hard.**
Regaining trust will be a long haul. Proceed to steps 5
through 7.

5 | **Be completely honest with your partner.**
Answer all questions and admit your wrongdoing fully.
Constantly reiterate how much you care for your partner. Your steadfastness and honesty is your only hope.
Gifts can be an essential part of making up, but mostly
you will have to put in a lot of time and energy to make
amends.

6 | **Do not give up on the relationship.**
Prepare yourself for many difficult conversations and
arguments. You will have to explain your true intentions
time and time again, and it may be a struggle even to
begin a conversation at times. Do not take the easy way
out. If kicked out of the house, do not leave easily; make
it clear that you are willing to struggle through whatever you are faced with to make the relationship work.

7 | **Avoid all contact with your former lover and
potential lovers.**
Never look at or discuss someone of the opposite sex
unless specifically asked to do so by your partner—and
even then, be cautious.

HOW TO STOP
A WEDDING

If the object of your affection is about to marry someone else, you need to act quickly to present your case
or forever hold your peace.

1 Make your feelings known before the service.
If you cannot appeal directly to the bride (or groom),
ask to speak to the officiant. The officiant should be
trained in how to handle such situations (go to step 4).

2 If you cannot stop the ceremony beforehand, wait
until the ceremony.
When you hear the officiant ask, "Does anyone know
a reason why these two people should not wed?" stand
up, say "I do," and approach the wedding party. (If you
do not wish to speak out, proceed to step 5.)

3 Ask the officiant if you can present your concerns in
private.

4 Present your objections.
The bride and groom will most likely join you and the
officiant for a consultation. If all agree with you (very
unlikely), the wedding will be halted. If the service
is to continue, respect the decision and leave immediately. Expect to be escorted from the premises.

Feigning a seizure will stop the ceremony.

5 If you do not have the courage to speak up during the ceremony, feign illness.

Fainting is a common occurrence at weddings, and faking it may not stop the ceremony. Instead, feign a seizure. Be sure to act before the vows are spoken. During the commotion while you are being carried out, insist on speaking with the officiant and then confess your feelings.

6 Pull the fire alarm.

If you cannot fake illness, pull the fire alarm. This will disrupt the ceremony, but will only delay the service until the alarm can be turned off. Use this time to speak with the officiant.

7 | If the ceremony has been completed, prevent the signing of the wedding license.

This is your last chance to prevent the marriage. Exchanging vows may make the marriage legitimate in the eyes of most people, but not necessarily in the eyes of the law. All states require a certificate of marriage signed by the officiant, bride, and groom. Traditionally, this document is not signed until after the service. Immediately after the ceremony, speak to the officiant and try to prevent the signing.

8 | If the license has been signed, try to prevent the marriage from being consummated.

In some states and in some religions, the marriage is not final until physical consummation. Find out where the bride and groom are planning to spend the first night and profess your love one last time. If that fails, your only hope is divorce.

HOW TO END A RELATIONSHIP

1 Get out immediately.

The moment you realize you are in—or starting to get into—a relationship that is not working for you, just say "no."

2 Decide on a mode of communication.

Voicemail, e-mail, or a card may be considered cowardly. However, these options have their advantages, particularly for a short-term relationship. If you are ending a long-term relationship, consider drafting a letter as a way to begin a conversation. Hand it to your partner to read while you are there.

3 Be kind.

Mention the things you like about your partner and express gratitude for the good times you have had together. This may seem contrived, but do it anyway.

4 State your position simply.

Be decisive, leaving no room for doubt or negotiation. It is not necessary for the other person to agree with you or to understand your reasons, but try to explain. One of the consequences of terminating a relationship is that you no longer have to get the other person to understand or agree.

5 Keep the focus on yourself.
Talk only about yourself, not the other person: Don't make it their fault. Say something simple and true, such as, "I prefer not to continue dating, but I want you to know how much I have enjoyed your sense of humor," or, "This relationship just is not working for me." If necessary, repeat these phrases.

6 Do not belabor the point.
You do not need to go over all the advantages and disadvantages of the relationship. Do not offer critical feedback or long explanations. If your real reason for breaking up might be painful for the other person to hear, do not mention it.

7 Do not try to take away the pain.
You are doing what is right for you and the other person has a right to a response. It is no longer your job to make the person feel better. Be firm but not cruel.

8 Never say, "I will call you."
When tossed out insincerely, this phrase is unimaginative and unkind. Instead, try saying something more honest and more final: "Maybe we will see each other again sometime. If not, have a nice life."

APPENDIX

THE "IT'S NOT YOU, IT'S ME" LETTER

Dear _____ ,

    I won't be able to make it this Saturday, or any Saturday, in fact. The truth is, I just can't be in a committed relationship right now. It's not you, it's me. I'm just not able to appreciate all that you have to give.

    I feel like we've been spinning our wheels these last few years / months / weeks / days. I can't believe how wonderful you've been to me and how much you've put up with. You deserve better. I can't put you through this anymore and I can't give you what you need / want / deserve right now. I need more space, and I need time to figure out who the real [*your name here*] is.

    It may take some time, but I hope we can still be friends.

Sincerely,

[*your name here*]

For short-term relationships, this letter may be sent via fax or e-mail.
To download the latest version, visit www.worstcasescenarios.com.

USEFUL EXCUSES

This never happened to me before.

I had a really tough day at work.

Not tonight, I have a meeting.

I have to get up early.

I'm too drunk.

I'm not drunk enough.

My turtle died.

I'm gay.

I'm straight.

I can't decide.

It's an old football injury.

I forgot my wallet.

I have to wash my hair.

My Aunt Flo is visiting.

I am leaving the country.

I need to take my medication.

I couldn't find a place to park.

I couldn't get a cab.

I left it in the cab.

I have to catch a plane.

I buy it for the articles.

They're supposed to test them at the factory.

Nobody's perfect.

I warned you about me.

We don't know each other well enough.

We know each other too well for that.

I didn't think you were coming back today.

He/she needed a friend.

It meant nothing to me.

Someone told me it was an art film.

We might learn some new things from it.

I have a bad back.

I have bad knees.

I asked you first.

I have to walk my dog.

That's not what I meant.

I don't remember saying that.

I'm terrible with names.

I can't bend over that far.

I didn't think you would notice.

My pager is broken.

My cell phone needs recharging.

My computer has a virus.

Your voicemail was full.

Your server must have been down.

I thought you meant next Friday.

It won't stain.

They're family.

I thought you understood without my having
    to say it.

Next time will be better.

PICKUP LINES TO AVOID

The human body is 90 percent water, and I'm real thirsty.

Can I buy you a drink or do you just want the money?

With a mane like that you must be a Leo.

Do you have a mirror in your pants? Because I can see myself in them.

Are your legs tired? Because you have been running through my dreams all night.

Is your father a thief? He has stolen the stars from the skies and put them in your eyes.

Are you okay? It must have been a long fall from heaven.

I really like that outfit. It would look great crumpled at the end of my bed.

What do you like to eat for breakfast? Oh good, I have that.

I know they say milk does a body good—but damn, how much have you been drinking?

So, are you legal?

I have cable TV.

If I told you that you have a lovely body, would you hold it against me?

Did the sun just come out or did you smile at me?

Is it hot in here, or is it just you?

Do you believe in love at first sight or do I have to walk by you again?

Hey, I lost my phone number . . . can I have yours?

If you were a burger at McDonald's, I'd call you McBeautiful.

Hi, my name's _____. But you can call me . . . tonight.

No wonder the sky's gray today—all the blue is in your eyes.

What's your name? Or shall I just call you mine?

If I could rearrange the alphabet, I'd put U and I together.

Look at you with all those curves and me with no brakes!

I may not be Fred Flintstone/Wilma Flintstone, but I can sure make your bed rock!

Do you have any raisins? No? How about a date?

Do you have a Band-Aid? 'Cause I skinned my knee when I fell for you.

Can I have a picture of you so I can show Santa what I want for Christmas?

My bed is broken. Can I sleep in yours?

I'm not feeling myself tonight. Can I feel you?

My name is _____. Remember that; you'll be screaming it later.

Is that a ladder in your stockings or the stairway to heaven?

I may not be the best looking guy/girl in here, but I'm the only one talking to you.

(*Lick finger and wipe on his/her shirt.*) Let's get you out of these wet clothes.

GUIDE TO BODY LANGUAGE

Good Signs

Leans in = receptiveness

Legs slightly apart = attraction

Makes good eye contact = sincerity

Matches your breathing = a meeting of the minds

Moves when you do = a good match

Holds palms open = receptiveness, an invitation

Parts lips = desire

Smiles with crow's feet = genuine amusement, attraction

Touches face, cheek = interest, attraction

Touches you = desire, attraction

Twirls hair = attraction, flirtation

Unbuttons jacket or shirt = comfort, interest

Bad Signs

Clenches jaw = impatience, anger

Crosses legs or arms = defensiveness

Holds finger to chin or lips = evaluation, criticism

Looks around = disinterest, boredom

Looks away = insincerity

Nods too much = disinterest, short attention span

Rubs neck or head = impatience, frustration

Rubs nose or eyes = dismissal, readiness to move on

Shifts weight = uncertainty, nervousness

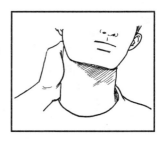

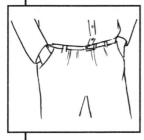

Shoves hands in pockets = feelings of inadequacy or insecurity, disinterest

Slouches = boredom, disinterest

Smiles without crow's feet = an attempt to look happy

THE EXPERTS

How to Determine If Your Date Is an Axe Murderer
Source: Julie Harmon, Ph.D., is executive director of IMPACT Safety Programs, a Columbus, Ohio–based nonprofit anti-violence organization with affiliates across the United States (1-800-345-KICK). With a background in psychology, she has worked for 25 years in various areas of anti-violence programming.

How to Determine If Your Date Is Married
Source: Pat Gaudette is an Internet publisher specializing in various aspects of relationships, including divorce and midlife crisis.

How to Determine the Gender of Your Date
Sources: Glenn Fitzpatrick, Ph.D., is an anthropologist based in Phoenix, Arizona, who has undertaken a study of physical differences between genders. • Linda Hunter is a private investigator and security specialist in Santa Barbara, California.

How to Determine If Your Date Is a Con Artist
Source: Julie Harmon, Ph.D.

How to Fend Off an Obsessive Ex
Source: Julie Harmon, Ph.D.

How to Fend Off a Pickup Artist
Source: Nancy Slotnick is the owner of Drip Café,

a New York City café with a dating service, and www.DripCafe.com, a national network of dating cafés.

How to Deal with a Date Who Moves Too Fast
Sources: Margaret Shapiro, MSW, is assistant director of the Pennsylvania Council for Relationships. She is a licensed clinical social worker in Massachusetts and Pennsylvania, and has been a practicing psychotherapist for 25 years. • Sarah Raskin is outreach and volunteer coordinator for Helpmate, a domestic violence service agency in western North Carolina. She provides educational sessions to professionals, civic groups, religious organizations, schools, government agencies, and other community groups.

How to Escape from a Bad Date
Source: Antonio J. Mendez is a retired CIA intelligence officer and the author of *The Master of Disguise: My Secret Life in the CIA*. For 25 years he worked undercover and has held various positions within the CIA, including Chief of Disguise and Chief of the Graphics and Authentication Division.

CHAPTER 2: FIRST IMPRESSIONS

How to Spot a Fake
Sources: Nicole Cummings is the founder of the world's largest online breast augmentation resource, Breast Augmentation and Breast Implants Information

by Nicole, at www.implantinfo.com. Her site has been featured in the *New York Times* and in the *Journal of the American Society of Plastic Surgeons*. She is the producer of an educational video, *Before and After Breast Augmentation*, which won a Telly Award. • Carliz S. Teague is CEO of 1stclasswigs.com, a website that provides wigs and hair accessories for men and women.

How to Survive a Fashion Emergency
Source: Karen Bressler is a New York City–based freelance writer, editorial director of fashionwindow.com, fashion columnist for *Ocean Drive* magazine, and co-author of *A Century of Lingerie*.

How to Treat a Pimple
Source: Dermatologist Jerome Aronberg is a fellow of the American Board of Dermatology and a past president of the Missouri State Dermatological Society. Currently, he is an assistant clinical professor of dermatology at Washington University in St. Louis. He is the author of *Caring for Your Skin with Over-the-Counter Drugs* and has contributed to *Shape* and *Glamour* magazines. Dr. Aronberg has a private practice in Clayton, Missouri.

How to Treat a Shaving Wound
Sources: Robert and Charlotte Johnston own the Barber Shop Trading Co., a men's store in the United Kingdom, www.barbershop.co.uk. • Dr. James Li practices and teaches in the Division of Emergency Medicine at Harvard Medical School in Cambridge,

Massachusetts. He is an instructor for the American College of Surgeons' course for physicians, Advanced Trauma Life Support.

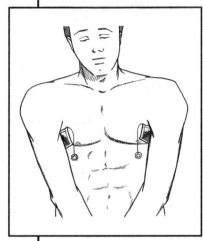

How to Deal with Body Odor
Sources: Maryann Bart is a homeopathic nurse and nutritionist who lives in Canton, Ohio. • Ginseng is a homeopathic drugstore based in Philadelphia, Pennsylvania.

How to Deal with Bad Breath
Sources: Mel Rosenberg, Ph.D., is a professor of microbiology at the Goldschleger School of Dental Medicine at Tel-Aviv University, where he heads the Laboratory for Oral Microbiology. He also holds positions with the University of Toronto Faculty of Dentistry and the University of Pennsylvania School of Dental Medicine. Dr. Rosenberg focuses on the diagnosis and treatment of oral malodor, and he has published more than ninety scientific articles, chapters, editorials, books, reviews, and patents in this area. • Richard Hafter, D.D.S., has practiced family dentistry in Hammonton, New Jersey, for 35 years. • Mehdi Kalani, M.D., is a surgeon, also in Hammonton, New Jersey.

CHAPTER 3: RESTAURANT AND BAR SURVIVAL SKILLS

How to Get an Emergency Reservation
Source: Phyllis Richman was the restaurant critic for the *Washington Post* for 23 years. She has written three mysteries featuring restaurant critic Chas Wheatley: *The Butter Did It, Murder on the Gravy Train*, and *Who's Afraid of Virginia Ham?*

How to Save Your Date from Choking
Source: Dr. James Li.

How to Survive If You Have Excessive Gas
Source: Liz Applegate, Ph.D., is a faculty member of the Nutrition Department at the University of California, Davis, and a recognized expert on nutrition and performance. She has written more than 300 articles for national magazines and is nutrition editor and columnist for *Runner's World* magazine. Dr. Applegate is the author of several books, most recently *Eat Smart, Play Hard.*

How to Survive If Your Credit Card Is Declined
Sources: Phyllis Richman (above), who does not recommend "dining and dashing" under any circumstances. • Jamie Hoffman is the general manager of Singer Equipment Company, a Pennsylvania-based restaurant supply company. He has been in the business for 18 years.

How to Fend Off Competitors for Your Date
Sources: Sherry Amatenstein is the author of *The Q & A Dating Book* and *Love Lessons from Bad Breakups*. She is the dating columnist for iVillage.com, conducts dating seminars around the country, and has appeared on numerous talk shows as a relationships expert. • Shawn Croft is Love & Dating correspondent for the largest online-only men's magazine, AskMen.com. He has a background in business, sociology, psychology, women's studies, and anthropology. He has also been a waiter and a bartender. • Dr. James Li.

How to Deal with a Drunken Date
Source: Kathy Hamlin has been a bartender at Mr. G's Lounge in Deltona, Florida, for 10 years. She is the Cocktails Guide at About.com and is the author of numerous articles on cocktails and cocktail history.

How to Sober Up Fast
Source: Kathy Hamlin.

How to Carry a Date Who Is Passed Out
Source: Vince Christopher is a physical therapist and amateur weight lifter who lives in New York City.

How to Survive If You Are Stopped by the Police
Sources: Attorneys Barry D. Kowitt and Kevin M. Unger are partners in the law firm of Unger & Kowitt, and have offices in Plantation and Miami, Florida. They have handled more than twenty thousand traffic tickets

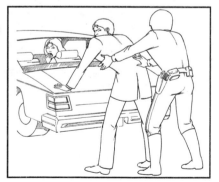

for clients. • Attorney Mel Leiding has been in private practice in California for 18 years and is the author of *How to Fight Your Traffic Ticket & Win!* He is a member of the experts' panel for the National Motorists Association, an advocacy group for motorists' rights. • Josh Herman owns Josh Herman Bail Bonds in Beverly Hills, California, and writes bail throughout the country. He has handled thousands of felony DUI cases and has written bail for numerous high-profile clients. The company is online at www.jhbail.com.

CHAPTER 4: BEDROOM SURVIVAL SKILLS

How to Deal with a Bad Kisser
Source: Carol Queen, Ed.D., is the staff sexologist at Good Vibrations in San Francisco. She is an author and sex educator who has written and edited several books, including *Exhibitionism for the Shy* and *Real Live Nude Girl: Chronicles of Sex-Positive Culture*.

How to Remove Difficult Clothing
Sources: Carol Queen, Ed.D. • Gilly Aroshas is the owner of Gilly Jeans Western Fashions in Phila-

delphia, Pennsylvania. He has been in business for 16 years and has been wearing cowboy boots for 35 years.

How to Fake an Orgasm
Source: Carol Queen, Ed.D.

How to Create Privacy If Your Door Does Not Lock
Source: Linda Hunter.

How to Have Sex in a Small Space
Sources: The Masked ScaVENger is a general safety engineering consultant and a member of the American Society of Safety Engineers. He uses this pseudonym to protect his identity. • Carol Queen, Ed.D.

How to Survive Snoring
Source: Jason H. Mateika holds a Ph.D. in physiology and is an assistant professor at Teachers College, Columbia University. He has been involved in sleep research since 1990 and is currently the director of the Sleep and Respiratory Physiology Laboratory at Teachers College.

How to Survive If You Wake Up Next to Someone Whose Name You Don't Remember
Source: Linda Hunter.

CHAPTER 5: RELATIONSHIP SURVIVAL

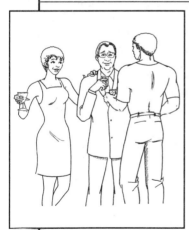

How to Survive If You Run into Your Ex
Source: Mary Mitchell is the author of six books on manners, and president of the Mitchell Organization, a Philadelphia-based corporate training company. She writes a syndicated newspaper column, "Ms. Demeanor," as well as columns for the Work channel of iVillage.com, under the moniker "Confidence Coach."

How to Survive Meeting the Parents
Source: Robin Thompson founded the Robin Thompson Charm School in 1983 and lectures on business etiquette and image at colleges, universities, and businesses throughout the country. She is the author of *Be the Best You Can Be* and runs etiquette-network.com.

How to Survive If You Forget a Birthday
Source: Mary Mitchell.

How to Deal with a Cheating Lover
Source: Margaret Shapiro, MSW.

How to Have an Affair and Not Get Caught
Sources: Mark Burns, Ph.D., is a licensed psychotherapist based in Seattle, Washington, who specializes in couples therapy. • *How to Have an Affair and Not Get Caught*, by Paul and Linda Lewis. • *How to Have an Affair and Never Get Caught*, by Jay D. Louise. • Debbie Layton-Tholl, Ph.D, is a clinical psychologist in Boca Raton, Florida, who specializes in extramarital affairs. She is a frequent speaker and lecturer on affairs and divorce.

How to Stop a Wedding
Source: Robin Thompson.

How to End a Relationship
Sources: Susan Page conducts relationship workshops and is the author of *If I'm So Wonderful, Why Am I Still Single?*; *Happily Married: The Eight Essential Traits of Couples Who Thrive*; *How One of You Can Bring the Two of You Together*; and *If We're So in Love, Why Aren't We Happy?* • Sherry Amatenstein.

ABOUT THE AUTHORS

JOSHUA PIVEN is the co-author (with David Borgenicht) of the best-selling *The Worst-Case Scenario Survival Handbook* series. He has been stood up, put down, lied to, and cheated on, but fortunately not by his wife. He lives in Philadelphia.

DAVID BORGENICHT is a writer, editor, and part-time lover whose turn-ons are candlelight dinners, stargazing, and women who aren't afraid of sharks. Turn-offs: sewage treatment plants, proboscis monkeys, and sucking chest wounds. He is the co-author, with Joshua Piven, of the best-selling *Worst-Case Scenario Survival Handbook* series, and lives in Philadelphia with his wife—a woman who is not only three times a lady, but who saved him from a life of dating hell.

JENNIFER WORICK is an editor and the author of *My Dysfunctional Life* and *My Fabulous Life* (Chronicle Books), as well as *Nancy Drew's Guide to Life*. She has dated a variety of motley men, including a fellow who was briefly trapped in a cult compound in upstate New York and a boyfriend who went weak in the knees whenever he heard Tears for Fears. She has also extricated herself without incident from a hotel room with the entire Wisconsin rugby team. She lives in Philadelphia and—at press time—is single.

BRENDA BROWN is a freelance illustrator and cartoonist whose work has appeared in many books and major publications, including *The Worst-Case Scenario Survival Handbook* series, *Reader's Digest*, the *Saturday Evening Post*, the *National Enquirer*, *Federal Lawyer*, and *National Review*. Her digital graphics have been incorporated into software programs developed by Adobe Systems, Deneba Software, Corel Corp, and many websites.

Check out www.worstcasescenarios.com for updates, new scenarios, and more! Because you just never know . . .

ACKNOWLEDGMENTS

The authors would like to extend their thanks and the promise of lifelong good karma to all of the experts who contributed their knowledge and experience to this project. Without you we are nothing—or at least a lot less knowledgeable.

Josh Piven thanks his wife, Christine, and his parents for their support.

David Borgenicht thanks Jay Schaefer, Steve Mockus, Jason Rekulak, Frances Soo Ping Chow, Brenda Brown, and the entire staff at Chronicle Books and Quirk Productions. He'd also like to apologize to everyone who dated him before his wife.

Jennifer Worick thanks Margy Dooley, Irv Furman, Robin Gorman Newman, Peter Gwin, Richard Marx, Jason Rekulak, Karen Salmonsohn, Kerry Tessaro, and Nan Troiano.

about the authors